Dear Bette: Advice From The Screen Queen

PATRICE WILLIAMS MARKS

PHOTOPLAY COMBINED WITH MOVIE MIRROR

Circa Publishing

With Love... Bette

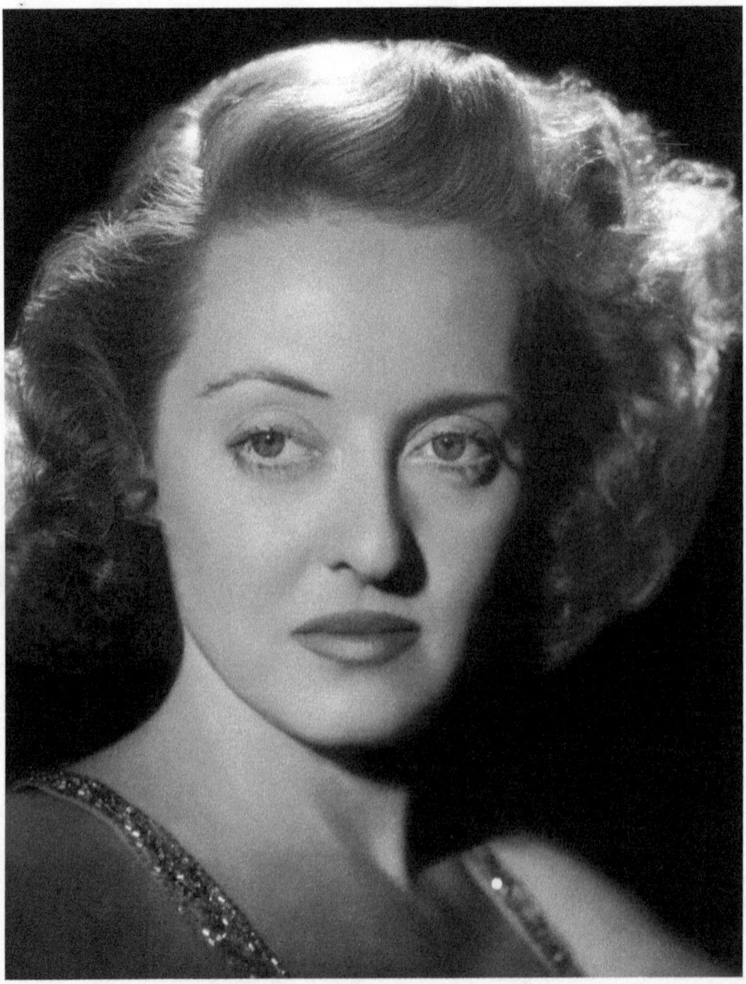

"I often think that a slightly exposed shoulder emerging from a long satin nightgown packs more sex than two naked bodies in bed." *Bette*

Dedicated to all the other saucy, trailblazing, box-demolishing Bette's out there.

Special Thanks

I wish I could personally thank each one of you for coming across my books and actually clicking on the BUY button. I hope I haven't disappointed any of you.

You are a major reason why I write. Sure I'd continue to write even if no one purchased a book, but it is a lot more satisfying to know that you actually enjoy following my characters on their rides. Email me and let me know: pwm@patricewilliams-marks.com

And before I forget, a special thank you to everyone who has taken a moment to REVIEW THIS BOOK.

Patrice Williams Marks

Bette Davis Eyes

UrbanDictionary.com:

1) Used to describe eyes that are prominent (i.e., eyes that sit forward in the face), very large and attractive like legendary actress Bette Davis.

2) A 1981 Number 1 hit single by Kim Carnes (it was the bestselling record of 1981).

Introduction

Bette Davis, one of the greatest American actresses (and legend) in cinematic history, was known for her drive to portray unsympathetic, unattractive, sardonic characters when others refused.

Bette was a badass bitch; a moniker she heard often in her life. Born April 5, 1908, on a Sunday, in Lowell, Massachusetts, Bette was known to seduce her leading men and leave her rivals in the dust.

Bette was extraordinary.

Neil Norman once wrote, "*She had weathered the storms of disfavor, flops and lawsuits – not to mention seeing off a quartet of husbands – resurrecting herself time and again to the point where she became a living legend. Death was not an option.*"

Yet, at the age of 81, while in Neuilly France, by invitation, she passed away from metastasized breast cancer.

Bette wasn't always a bulldozer in heels. After her parents divorced, Bette was raised by her very strict mother, Ruth, and lived with her and her sister, Barbara.

She took drama courses in school and acted in plays. Once she graduated, she was not encouraged to pursue the acting profession as she was not considered, "*beautiful*." But Bette knew better.

She moved to New York, took more classes, landed bit parts and pushed forward.

She eventually was given several screen tests, though executives were not impressed.

At this time, Bette was inexperienced, repressed and uncomfortable around young men. Once, when a young actor named Henry Fonda innocently kissed 17-year-old Bette on her cheek, she thought she was, "*with child.*" She assumed that she was engaged to Fonda from that moment on.

But, as we know, that innocence was soon lost. Bette was single-minded in her pursuit of stardom, even if that meant she had to put love, family and happiness on hold.

And she found it.

But what she lost... was monumental.

By the time she reached the age of 32, she was supporting her mother, sister, husbands, (prior and present), had a drinking problem and had several abortions. Bette was a complicated force of nature, and only a few could hold on for the ride.

You can now see why many clambered to get her advice on their most personal and private matters.

Bette was blunt, rarely diplomatic. But she spoke the truth with finesse. Fans would write to PhotoPlay magazine from 1935-1948 seeking her advice, and Bette responded.

Some of these letters are sweet, funny; some gut-wrenchingly sad, while others are obnoxious.

They are reprinted intact without any edits.

Enjoy.

Contents

Letters... xv

Epilogue 1

About The Author 3

Letters...

"This month I decided to do my bit toward answering that perennial question, "How Can I Become An Actress" in its several phases. I have selected representative letters out of the thousands that come in every month, asking approximately the same questions, and I hope my answers will prove to be useful. This is the first."

Bette Davis

Dear Miss Davis:

You are a busy woman, of course. I've read that over and over again. But, Miss Davis, if you don't answer my letter I think I am going to hate you forever.

You are supposed to be such a Good Samaritan, and now is your chance to prove it. I have a wonderful little daughter who is just 4-years-old. Her name is Deanna, named after Deanna Durbin.

She is a very unusual little girl who can learn poems and remember them indefinitely. She has a natural talent for singing and dancing and I know there is a place in motion pictures for her.

Now, here is my problem. My husband died two years

ago and since that time I have been working in a department store, barely getting by. I don't have any extra cash with which to give Deanna the training she needs.

That's where you come in. Could you loan me the money to come to Hollywood, or go to New York, and pay a good teacher to give my baby the start in life she deserves? When she becomes famous you will have the satisfaction of claiming her as a protégée, and at that time she will pay you back every penny.

I am planning on hearing from you real soon.

From a desperate mother.

M.I.

Dear Min. M.I.:

I am not answering your letter because you threaten to hate me forever if I don't reply. After all, hatred takes a lot of time and energy and you really haven't any to spare since you are working so hard and taking care of your small girl.

I am answering your letter because those people who are in the motion - picture industry receive thousands of similar letters every day. If you were in our shoes, you would understand how impossible it is for us to grant such requests: think of Santa Claus- even he is expected to operate only one night in an entire year. All of us are asked a hundred times a day for gifts. And surely you haven't forgotten all the myriad other demands upon us — taxes, benefits, charities, donations by the dozens. We love to respond, of course, but we are only human and the extent of our salaries is widely misunderstood.

Now, about your little girl. She sounds like a darling. However, in my humble opinion, for parents to start letting children earn their way at such a tender age is shameful. Extreme talent is very rare and every year there are thousands of parents and children who are disappointed because vast sums of money have been spent on training and in the final selection, only one child achieves stardom, whereas the others fall back into the ranks of the unknowns. This results, frequently, in a permanent mental hurt to the child; his entire personality may be changed. It seems to me that all parents should guard against setting up hopes and dreams in a child's heart, which may only be destroyed.

You sign yourself as, "desperate mother." I don't wish to be unkind, but no woman should use the future of her child to overcome desperation. That is a job she must do for herself.

Yours truly,
BETTE DAVIS

Dear Miss Davis:

I can scarcely wait until your picture "Now, Voyager" comes to our town. I never miss a Bette Davis picture. That brings me to something I would like to ask you: How to become a movie star?

I guess I'd rather be frank. I'm no prize. I am five feet eight inches tall and I weigh about a hundred and thirty pounds. My hair is just plain brown and my eyes are blue with thick lashes. I have quite a lot of freckles; I would wear cold cream at night except that my two older sisters who sleep in the same room with me make fun of me.

I would like to get away from home and become famous just to show them I'm not such a goon. I know that being an actress is no snap and I'm willing to slave for a chance to prove that I can really act.

A Plain Jane

Dear "Plain Jane:"

Goodness, why do you describe yourself like something that would scare Bela Lugosi? After all, five feet eight inches of height isn't so tall; Alexis Smith is your height. As for freckles, Myrna Loy has always been proud of hers. If you want to wear cold cream at night, ignore your sisters' teasing. When they discover that they no longer get a rise out of you, they will forget it

Unfortunately, wanting to become famous to prove to your family that you aren't a "goon" as you say, isn't the right approach to becoming an actress. As you must realize, there are no rules about appearances alone making a star; we have every type of face in Hollywood. Also, success in pictures is not always a question of hard work—there are so many other things to consider.

It seems to me that your problem is first to learn to look well-groomed all the time. Keep your hair brushed, your complexion clear and your dresses neat. Walk with your shoulders back and stop hating yourself. Once you have won the respect of everyone in your town, let the future develop as it will.

Sincerely yours,
BETTE DAVIS

Dear Miss Davis:

I think you are the most wonderful actress in the world and I hope I will be just like you someday. That is why I am writing to you.

For the last three years, ever since I was graduated from high school, I have been working in our local telephone exchange. At first I thought that the job would allow me enough time to drive to a town forty miles away and I try to do something over the radio because everyone says I have a very beautiful speaking voice and I can sing a little although I've never had lessons.

However, you know what has happened. The men have all gone into the Army and girls who could leave home have gone to larger cities where there are defense plants, so the first thing I knew I was working like mad just to take care of the business of our local exchange.

I did one smart thing - I saved my money. I now have five hundred dollars in the bank and I have been thinking seriously of coming to Hollywood and trying to get a break in pictures. I thought maybe I could work on a studio switchboard and my voice would give me a chance at screen test. I am not bad-looking. My hair is naturally curly and chestnut in color, my eyes are greenish, and my skin is good and clear.

What do you think, Miss Davis?

Yours very truly,

M

Dear Miss M:

You sound like a sensible, levelheaded girl. Yes, if I were you, I would go either to Hollywood or to New York. I say this only because you have five hundred dollars tucked away for emergencies; better keep that much and hold onto your present job until you have enough for carfare and a wardrobe that will last at least six months.

Any girl over twenty-one who is able to run a large switchboard and who has five hundred dollars as anchor against ill winds is justified in trying her luck with a career.

Yours truly,

BETTE DAVIS

Dear Miss Davis:

Because I have read such nice things about your friendliness to ambitious newcomers, I am taking the liberty of bringing my problem to you.

I am seventeen years old, a senior in high school. I have taken singing lessons since I was thirteen and I have had the luck to sing over several radio stations.

I am five feet four inches tall and I weigh 110 without dieting. My hair is naturally curly and deep auburn in color and my eyes are dark blue.

Probably you are thinking, "that conceited little drip," but I'm not really.

I know that I don't know a single thing about dramatic technique and I know it would be silly to try to get into pictures without training. My family wants me to finish my high-school work and take a year or two at our State University and I think I would do as they wish.

What I would like to have you tell me, Miss Davis, is this: What can I do now to begin fitting myself for a stage and movie career? Are there some home exercises I could do to improve my dictation? What sort of books ought I to read?

I know how frightfully busy you are. Could you have your secretary give me some sort of outline that I should follow for the next three years? I know that sounds pretty presumptuous, but writing to you is the only way I could think of, in which I could get the real lowdown.

Thanking you with my whole heart,
Yours sincerely,
Margaret B

Dear Margaret B:

Please don't feel that you have been "a conceited little drip"— as you say— because of telling me how you look. As a matter of fact, you sound very attractive. One of the most important things in life is to feel attractive, if you really are. Beauty is nothing over which to be conceited, because it is something over which the individual has no control—it is a happy act of nature.

I like your letter because it shows an intelligent approach to your ambition. And there are many things you can do now to further your chances of realizing that ambition.

You are quite right in planning to attend a university if your parents wish you to do so. However, between now and then you will no doubt be given many opportunities to appear before the public and something unusual may occur to change your plans.

No doubt there is some sort of dramatic class in your high school. You should join, if possible, and appear in as many plays as possible. You should read as many plays as you can, because this will give you a feeling for great lines in dramas.

Perhaps there is a competent dancing teacher in or near your town. I think you should take lessons, not so much with the idea of becoming a dancer, as to learn how to handle your body with grace and poise.

Meanwhile, the most important thing for you to do is to work on your speaking voice and your diction. There are- certain definite rules about voice placement which would have to be explained to you by a teacher, I think. However, there are two excellent books available on the subject, "Phonetic Studies In Folk Speech," by Anne Darrow and, "The Speaking Voice" by Amelia Summerville.

You must have noticed that a pleasant speaking voice is a prime asset in any walk of life and that good diction is a treasure unpossessed by many, many people.

Having attained grace and a flexible, compelling voice during the next three years, you will have taken a long step toward success in any field.

Yours truly,
BETTE DAVIS

Dear Bette Davis Farnsworth:

Can you sing? I guess you can't, because I have never heard you, but you sure can act. You can act Romantic, you can act serious, you can act Comic, and several other kinds.

I can't act for sour apples. But I can sing. I am the ambitious one - I want to sing with an orchestra. My voice is blue, but it also has a lovely high range, as the leader of our church choir told me.

Please tell me how I can start out to get a chance to sing with an orchestra. Do you have friends who are orchestra leaders? Could you introduce me to one, or could you please tell me how to get started?

Yours in the groove,

Joann A.

Dear Joan A.:

If you are really interested in checking up on my singing voice, you might watch for a picture titled, "Thank Your Lucky Stars" in which I actually do something that is called singing. You might let me know how successful the effort was, after you have seen the picture.

In the first place, it seems to me that you should secure several other opinions about your voice, in addition to that of your choir leader. Is there a vocal teacher in your town? If so, why don't you sing for him or her and secure that impression?

If there is a radio station near your home, why don't you try to arrange for an audition? In case some trained radio authority thinks your voice is really fine enough to merit attention, he will undoubtedly direct you to a good teacher. The value of being taught by someone who understands the human voice is that the voice is a delicate instrument and you can ruin it by treating it badly. You should learn to use it properly.

Once you have had training, you will hear of some, "name" band on tour near your home. At that time you should try to make arrangements for an audition by the leader. The best of luck to you.

Sincerely.

Bette Davis.

DEAR MISS DAVIS:

You must know practically everyone of importance in Hollywood, so I am writing to you for some information.

I don't know whether you have ever heard of this small town in which I live or not - probably not, as we aren't famous for anything. There are railroad shops here, however, and my father is one of the foremen and makes a pretty good salary. He wants me to have the advantages that girls in larger towns have, but I don't want anything except a chance at Hollywood.

Now here is my problem, Miss Davis. There is a man who stops here in town occasionally. I met him first at the drugstore one afternoon when he said I had the most beautiful profile he'd ever seen. I do have fairly regular features, so that doesn't exactly bond me over, but when he said that my hair was a perfect color for the Technicolor camera and that my entire face and body were photogenic, I began to get interested.

This man says he is a talent scout for a major studio and he wants me to drive out to Hollywood with him. My mother has met him and thinks he is a nice, courteous young man, but she thought we shouldn't tell my father about my opportunity as he is always getting suspicions.

Miss Davis, could you give me the names of the accredited talent scouts in my state, or in my section of the country? I trust this man and he seems like a wonderful person, what I am not sure I want to go on a wild goose chase to Hollywood and find out that he hasn't any real influence, when we get there.

Thank you so much for your help.

Mady J.

Dear Mady J.:

Naturally, it isn't possible for me to supply the names of all accredited talent scouts. They change from time to time, of course, and there are other good reasons for not broadcasting their presence in a particular locality.

However, a talent scout should be able to supply you instantly with the name of his studio. He should carry complete identification. If you will send me this man's name, I will find out promptly whether he is employed by any of our major studios.

One word of advice to you, Mady, and to all girls tempted by Hollywood offers... don't believe anything you hear unless the man can prove himself to your local banker.

My candid impression is that this man is not trustworthy.

Yours truly,

BETTE DAVIS

Dear Miss Davis:

I am confiding in you because you are a woman and with your great heart you may be able to help me to escape my grief.

I am from a small town in Louisiana. I was married to a very dear and sweet girl in November, 1941. We were so happy and we loved each other so dearly! We expected our baby in September, 1942. We had hoped for a little girl and we had named her Dolores Elaine. We had all kinds of dreams and plans for her; we bought so many pretty clothes and had everything ready.

On Friday night, September 18, 1942, I had to take her (my wife) to a clinic in town. The next morning the baby was born, a darling little girl with curly red hair. She only lived about twenty minutes, even though she weighed eight and a half pounds.

I have dark red curly hair and we wanted that baby to have curly red hair and it did. It was about 7:30 in the morning that my baby died and it hit me so hard I cried and cried; I couldn't think of a way to tell my wife. Finally I just couldn't do it; my mother-in-law had to tell her. Well. Peaches (that was my wife) took it like a swell little soldier. About 11:30 she began to fail. The doctor called an ambulance to rush her to a near-by city, but after we had driven about forty miles she opened her eyes and looked at me. She said. "I see you, honey. Don't ever leave me. I love you so much and will always be with you wherever you go." Then she was gone forever.

I decided to go into the Marine Corps, as life there isn't so long. I have been in about a year—a year of torture to my mind. At night I dream of her as we used to be; I dream of her lying down there in her coffin. All day long I think of her no matter what I am doing. When I eat, I think of the things she liked. Sometimes I think I am just plain going nuts.

Please tell me some way to work at bringing myself together. I am only twenty years old. But I feel three times that age. Please answer me and tell me how to go on living.
Tom F.

Dear Private F:

I feel more than complimented that you feel I might be able to help you through this more difficult time in your life.

The only suggestion I have to offer is that you not worry about how not to think of your wife. Be glad that you want to. Also, be glad that your life with her was such an ideal one. This you can be very grateful for.

I think now you are inclined to be morbid about it. Remember with pleasure your life together, carry on your life as she would want you to. Keep busy. Do a good job for your country and have faith that lime will lessen the enormity of your immediate grief. I feel certain it will.

My sincere sympathy,
Bette Davis.

Dear Miss Bette Davis:

Can you help me with some good advice?

I have been married for seven months. I love my husband dearly, although I had to leave him once because of his jealousy. However, he's the one for me, so I came back.

My problem is that I love children and I want to have a child. My husband hates children. I have talked and talked, trying to make him see that a home without a child is no home at all. He has given me the excuse that he is afraid of being taken into the Army and both for his sake and my own, he didn't want a child. Now he has been classified 4F, but he still doesn't want children.

Can you think of some way in which I can convince him that the light of a home is a child?

Mrs. F. T.

Dear Mrs. F. T.:

The reason for your husband's unwillingness to have children is clearly defined in your letter: You state that he is so jealous of you and that you had to leave him during the early days of your marriage.

No doubt he is also jealous that a child might supplant him in your affection.

This is not an unusual situation. Many husbands resent and fear the coming of children because of the constant care and attention that must be lavished on a baby, leaving a husband to get along without the attentions a childless wife can administer.

There is only one way to get around this, I believe. If you have a friend who has a small child, or a relative, and you can teach the child to go to your husband to have toys fixed, or a shoe lied, or a story told, your husband might become so interested that he would decide that children are, as you say, "the light of a home."

However, if I know anything about men, I would fudge that he will have to come to this decision of his own free will. If you were to have a child otherwise, I feel, under the circumstances, you would be doing the child a great injustice. Your husband's jealousy might affect its entire life.

Bette Davis.

Dear Bette:

Really, Miss Davis, if you can't help me I don't know what I'll do.

I'm sixteen, but look twenty. I'm not especially pretty, but I have a merry smile and a nice disposition. I enjoy dancing and have been a hostess at dances for soldiers at a near-by Army camp. They are very respectable dances and my parents saw no harm in them. Frequently my mother was a senior hostess.

I met there a soldier named Bill. I saw him on five different occasions before he asked me for a date. As my mother thought he was nice. I accepted, then began to go steady with him. After four months, my friends took it for granted that we were practically engaged and I was in seventh heaven.

Then one night Bill said casually that his wife and baby were coming for a visit. You can't guess how thunderstruck and brokenhearted, I was not only for myself, but for Bill's wife who had also been cheated.

Well, the talk spread. Everybody thought Bill's wife would sue for divorce and name me. My reputation was ruined, but I went to Bill's wife and told her everything. We had never been introduced, but we understood each other instantly and she forgave me.

Now I am snubbed by people who were once my best friends. I have quit going to dances and I just sit home and read, trying to live down the shame I brought upon myself and my parents.

Please. Miss Davis, tell me if I have ruined my life completely. What should I tell myself when I turn sick with humiliation? How can I win back my friends?

Eunice R.

Dear Miss R:

In the first place, you did not bring shame upon yourself and your parents'. If anyone was guilty of any shame, it was Bill, who should have told you that he was married. Your only mistake, as I see it, was in assuming that you and Bill were engaged when he had not, obviously, asked you to marry him. However, you certainly aren't the first girl in the world to take a man more seriously than he intended.

It was splendid of you to go to Bill's wife and explain the situation.

Now you should forget the entire episode. If you ignore it and go on about your business as if nothing had happened, your friends will soon forget, too.

At sixteen, these things seem frightfully serious. At seventeen, you'll be thinking of some other boy – wait and see!

Bette Davis

Dear Miss Davis:

My case is this: I was engaged to a lieutenant in the Naval Air Corps when he crashed. By the grace of God, he escaped with his life although he underwent a three-hour operation.

When he began to recuperate, he refused to see me. I am attending college in a town about forty miles from his base; I keep in touch with him through his best friend. He does not want to see me as there is some doubt as to whether he will ever fly again.

I have received numerous letters from him since that time and in each letter he insists that things can never be the same again. Knowing him as I do, I feel sure he is sacrificing his own happiness to keep me from regretting any action I might take.

What can I do, or how may I prove to him that his condition makes no difference to me? If he can never fly again, I want to help rebuild his life on the ground. If he cannot walk, I want to help him build some sort of suitable career. So, should I go to see him against his wishes? How may I gain his understanding? Do you think I should hold him to our engagement?

Una K.

Dear Miss K:

The first thing to do is to determine whether your fiancé still loves you or not. You might ask some friend of his candidly to tell you the truth. Perhaps he is trying to break off your engagement in this way, so as not to hurt you.

On the other hand, he may be sacrificing himself, as you say. Once you have become convinced that he is still in love with you and that he wants to see you again, by all means take a chance and ignore his orders to stay away.

If you could talk to him, perhaps you could persuade him that nothing matters if you love someone. Your problem is going to be that of many, many girls before this war is over and it can only be solved - it seems to me - by devotion., understanding and a great deal of patience.

Bette Davis

My Dear Miss Davis:

My husband was in the service when we met and he was a good soldier at the time. We were married, after postponing it several times, and because of our deep love for one another, he placed his duty second. He overstayed his leave nearly thirty days. During all this time I was working. Every day I left him with his promise to go back to camp, only to come home and find him still there.

Finally he did return, only to be court-martialed and sentenced to twenty-three days. When he got out, he vowed he had had enough and would never do it again. He came home on week-end pass, then only "reported"—as he put it—occasionally. He said they had nothing for him to do in the Army. I didn't exactly believe him, but when I questioned him he would break down and cry, saying, "Okay, honey, if you don't believe me, what can I do?"

By that time I knew I was going to have a baby and I was so sick I had to stop work. Because my husband was getting no money—he said there was some sort of a misunderstanding in the payroll department— my sister kept us. She and her husband had good jobs. However, they went back East so I turned to the Red Cross.

All this time my husband and I were more in love than ever and so happy over the baby being on its way, but I couldn't get him to admit that he was a deserter. By this time I was almost positive, yet when questioned he always seemed to go to pieces. He was never brutal—just sort of beaten by life.

One night he didn't come home for dinner. The baby was then a month old, the dearest little girl on earth. I was crazy with worry, so I finally called the Bureau of Missing Persons. I learned that my husband had been picked up in civilian clothes while he was waiting for a friend who had been in the guardhouse with him—to hold up a store.

Now he has to pay a penalty for his mistakes. I'm

paying for them, too. I know my husband isn't really bad - it's just circumstances. All his life he has been kicked around. His father was mean to him. They always lived in poverty and he had a very slim education—no real chance. I can see why he deserted the Army, but I can't understand his turning to crime except that he loved me and the baby too much and had to find some way of supporting us.

All the time he was at home he did all of the work—dishes, cooking, washing, ironing, etc.—for otherwise I might have lost the baby. He even did all the diapers after she was born.

Miss Davis, am I foolish to hang on to this man even if I do love him so terribly? When he gets out in several years, should I be waiting, or what? Please help me.

Mrs. Roger M.

Dear Mrs. M:

Of course you aren't foolish to stand by your husband. Since you obviously love him and want to wait for him, that is the thing for you to do.

Of course, yours is the perfect example of letting a bad situation continue until it has developed into an inextricable tangle. If, as soon as you suspected that your husband was a deserter, you had talked to him about your suspicions – perhaps, all this aftermath could have been avoided. In wartime, no man in uniform can place any person above his duty.

However, your husband seems to be a man of gentle character. My feeling is that if you stand by him when he is released he will be able to return to normal living, working and building a future for you and your daughter.

Bette Davis

Dear Miss Davis:

I am seventeen-years-old and I have something on my mind that is driving me crazy. I have just been told that the woman I have believed to be my mother all these years, really isn't my mother at all. Miss Davis, you don't know what it means to look at a woman you have loved all your life, as a mother, and say to yourself. "That is not my mother."

This is what I have been told: That Mom took my brother and me when we were very small—so small that I don't remember a thing. My real father and mother couldn't find work, so they left our state after giving up their children. They have never been heard from since.

My brother was such a bad boy, they say, that Mom gave him up to an asylum and he was adopted by someone she doesn't know. She has no idea where my brother is.

When I ask Mom for more details she looks funny and won't answer me. Miss Davis, don't you think she should tell me everything she knows? Don't I have the right to know what my real name is? Don't I have a right to try to find my older brother? I might be crazy about him. What would you do if you were a girl in my place?

GRACE C.

Dear Miss C.,

If I were in your place, I would let well enough alone. You say that you might be crazy about this unknown lost brother of yours. That is true, of course, but you also might dislike him intensely.

You remind me a little of Pandora, the little Greek girl who was entrusted—probably remember from your mythology —with a box. She couldn't restrain her curiosity, to open the box and released all the trouble into the world. Actually, you have no idea what sort of difficulty you might be developing for yourself by prying into something that your adopted mother considers better locked away.

Have you stopped to consider that you may be causing your adopted mother a great deal of anguish? She must love you very dearly; by now she must feel that you are as much her daughter as if you were her own.

It seems to me that you owe her all the love and gratitude in the world. And no questions asked— I would trust her judgment in the matter.

Bette Davis.

Dear Miss Davis:

Can you please give me some good advice? I'll soon be twenty.

One boy I go with is in the Marine Corps (he's twenty-one); the other boy is in the Army Air Corps and will soon be twenty.

Both have asked me to marry them several times and although it seems impossible, I really and truly love both of them. I've known both for about five years and when I wasn't out with one. I'd be out with the other. Both are tall and blond. Neither has much of a trade, but both are very handy at doing everything.

Don't say I don't love either, because that won't be true. I know there could never be anyone beside these two. I've told both of them they would have to wait until after the war for an answer, but both are very anxious to know now. The one because he wants to decide what kind of a war job to take, a very dangerous one or a "ground crew" job. The other one because he's in a very dangerous Pacific zone and doubts if he'll come back, although he writes that he'll try his darnedest.

It all sounds very silly, but when you come right down to it it's all very serious. I'm selfish, I know, because I really want both, but seeing I can't have both, I want one of them —no one else.

This is the queerest mixup I've ever been in and it's been going on for years. Everyone says I'm a very levelheaded, capable person and I hold a responsible job in a large office, but my private life doesn't seem to be conducted very capably.

What would you do in my place?

Marilyn J.

Dear Miss J:

Your problem doesn't sound at all silly to me. You aren't the first girl in the world to admire two men at the same time with equal affection.

As you say you have already told both boys that they will have to wait until after the war for an answer. I think you have handled this as it should be. You are only twenty and who knows how long a time is going to elapse until we are finally victorious? A great many things can happen to change your opinions of even your two beaux. Although it doesn't seem possible to you now, you might even meet a third man who would solve your problem.

Why don't you continue to see both boys whenever they are on leave, and to write to them. But never marry until there is only one man you love more than any other you know.

Bette Davis.

Dear Miss Davis:

You'll think a service man "nuts" for writing to you, but I can't help it.

I want to tell you something. Last June 7, I met a young woman at a dance. She and I had an enjoyable evening and a late supper. For two months we dated every Saturday and once in a while I would see her during the week.

Then it happened. We quarreled. She is going with a crowd who think the only way to enjoy life is by constant spending. I am, shall I say, a very idealistic person and I know what life is, although I am only twenty.

I love her very much and I want the inspiration that comes from a woman's love. When we have mail call I watch, oh so closely, the light in the eyes of my fellow service men as they read the letters from their wives or sweethearts. I haven't any letter from this girl and I feel lost in a world of chaos.

She still has the attitude that money can buy the only thing in life.

How wrong is she?

George W.

Dear Private W:

Frankly, I think that you have taken an interest in a girl who is not the right one for you. When you state that she has the attitude that money can buy the only thing in life worthwhile and ask me how wrong this girl is, I can answer that in one word: Entirety.

Never have any illusion that marriage would reform a girl with such a viewpoint. If you could give her everything she wanted, she would make life miserable both for herself and you.

Why don't you wait until the war is over before you try to select a wife?

Bette Davis

Dear Bette Davis:

You may think it strange of me, asking you this. I have very short eyelashes. I have brown eyes and brown hair and I think if I had longer eyelashes it would improve the looks of my eyes.

Could you tell me how you and other movie actresses grow such long eyelashes?

Gayle C.

Dear Mrs. C:

The truth of the matter is that very few of us have the luxuriant eyelashes we appear to possess. I might say that, in this respect at least, the majority of us owe a great deal to the make-up artist.

However, there are a number of things that you can do to make your eyelashes appear thicker and to make them grow.

A good mascara, carefully applied, will give your lashes body and castor oil applied sparingly each night should do wonders toward encouraging growth.

Bette Davis

Dear Miss Davis:

I am an eighteen-year-old boy in the Coast Artillery. I am six-feet-tall, weigh 180 pounds and am neat and well-groomed. I believe my physical appearance is suitable to either stage or screen work with the exception of one thing—my two front teeth have a slight space between them and the enamel is a little bit mottled.

I have asked many dentists to remove the stain (which, incidentally, was caused by a mineral and fluorine content in drinking water) but they have told me that if they remove the stain the process will ruin the teeth.

Miss Davis, could you please recommend a good dentist? After this war is done I am going to a prominent dramatic school in California, but I fear that unless I get these teeth fixed, it will tend to ruin my chances. After all, an actor has to have a handsome smile.

Private Marlow F.

Dear Private F:

I spoke to a dentist about your problem and he assured me that fluorosis is quite common in large areas of Southern Colorado and Texas. Here is something very interesting: It seems that the same minerals in the drinking that cause discoloration also serve to form extremely hard, beautifully shaped teeth.

For this reason you are uniquely fortunate, because the discoloration and separation won't interfere with your stage or movie chances. In pictures, actors or actresses who don't have perfect teeth can obtain porcelain caps. These are featherweight and can be applied during working hours. You need have no worries that your teeth will be a handicap.

Bette Davis

In studying and answering the letters that you, the readers of Photoplay-Movie Mirror send me, Miss Dudley and I were inclined to believe at first that women had a priority on the problems of life.

However, I feel certain that many men have troubles about which they would like to write and I can assure them that their letters, if published, will cause them no embarrassment as all identification will be removed. May I add that those letters that we have already received from men have been exceptionally interesting—as you will see from this month's sample.

Bette

Dear Miss Davis:

I have read in Photoplay-Movie Mirror that you help people with their problems. Mine is a very serious one. I am a girl of eleven. I have recently found out by some letters I read that my mother has been going out with another man.

I would like to know if I should tell my father or keep the secret to myself.

Sincerely yours.

Suzanne H.

Dear Suzanne:

What you believe you have found out may or may not be true. However, you most assuredly have no right to discuss what you think you have discovered about your mother with your father.

In justice to your mother, remember that you are only eleven and that your mother may have many reasons for not having taken you into her confidence yet. She may have planned to talk over her plans or her problems with you when you are a little older.

In your letter you did not explain how it happened that you were reading your mother's letters. I would judge that she knows nothing about your prying into her affairs. There is an old saying that, 'eavesdropper never hears good of themselves.' I think it is also true that those who pry never discover pleasant news.

It seems to me that the information you have is not rightfully yours. Also, you may have misunderstood what you think you learned. I would say that this is a secret that you must keep to yourself until you are much older, or until your mother discusses it with you.

Sincerely,

Bette Davis

Dear Bette Davis:

You scorn so sweet and down-to- earth in the answers you have given other troubled readers that I am emboldened to bring my puzzle to you.

Forgive the seeming egotism of what follows, but I must equip you with some knowledge of myself if you are to answer me truly. I have read somewhere that judgment is only as accurate as preceding information.

So then, to the details: I have fallen head over heels in love with a man fifteen years my junior. He is a young Naval officer and I have long been the widow of a man of great prominence in our state. My husband, who died after three years of marriage, when I was twenty-five, was fifteen years older than I. An odd coincidence, isn't it?

My interests (I am now thirty- seven) are all extremely young. I can dance until dawn and feel fresh the next day; I ride horseback with enough ability to have won several jumping contests; I have the means to keep myself exceedingly well-dressed and well-groomed. My health is of the best.

Can you tell me, please, if—from your observations—there would seem to be any chance for happiness in a union between this man and myself. He is astonishingly mature for his years; I had judged him to be perhaps thirty-two or thirty-three when we first met. Not until he declared his love and asked me to marry him did I learn his actual age. My pride, at that moment, was too great to allow me to admit my age to him—he thinks I am about twenty-seven, as do my friends.

Would you, if you were I, tell him the truth, Miss Davis? And would you marry him?

Adelaide McM.

Dear Mrs. McM:

Yes, I believe you should tell this man about your age. We all know that nothing not based on a light can survive. Wouldn't it be far better for you to give him this information in advance of your marriage than for him to learn the truth for himself instead of from your friends later on?

If the difference in your ages matters a great deal to him, it is better to find that out at once. However, if it makes no difference to him, you have an excellent chance for a very happy marriage. It is well known that some men, particularly men who are mature for their years, prefer a woman of poise and excellence. I have known of several cases in which the woman's being older than the man has been a contributing factor in a successful marriage.

Sincerely yours,
Bette Davis

Dear Miss Davis:

I am asking your advice, because - as an important member of the movie community - you probably know best how to handle one of your associates.

Eight years ago, when I was nineteen, I was the victim of an unhappy marriage. I have but one beautiful reality left of that marriage—my seven-year-old son.

I am still considered very beautiful at twenty-seven. Now, Miss Davis, problem was: while I was lying in a hospital with a nervous breakdown, I heard a voice on the radio that seemed to be speaking directly to me.

The voice belonged to a famous bandleader-actor, who has made several pictures since that time, and of course he's a bachelor. I wrote to him while I was in the hospital and to my surprise he answered. We kept up a correspondence until four months ago when a relative of mine, who is the mother of grown children and past forty, attended one of this man's broadcasts and pretended she was I. To her it seemed like a very clever prank.

She laughed afterward and said this young man was astounded, so that he could hardly speak. Heaven only knows what he thinks. He probably feels that all my letters were lies and since that night I haven't heard from him.

I feel lost, because, you see, I am in love with him. I'm a sentimentalist and I know he is too, but how can I clear up this horrible mess without letting him think I am running after him?

Unhappy yours,
Jean W.

Dear Mrs. W:

It seems to me that you don't need to worry about this man's thinking that you are running, after after, when you wrote your first letter to him, you indicated that you were interested in him to the extent that you would make the first friendly overtures.

There are a great many charming instances in which intense romances have existed entirely in letters between two persons. George Bernard Shaw's love affair with Ellen Terry was carried on totally by mail. Elizabeth Barrett corresponded with Robert Browning long before they met. So, obviously, you need not apologize for having exchanged letters with this man.

I imagine that you are a little embarrassed at the thought that when you write and tell him the truth of what happened - as you surely should - he is going to realize that you must have told your relatives a good deal about your corresponding friendship. That is where you made your mistake - in telling too many other people about the letters.

However, you will be doing the man a great favor, it seems to me, if you will again write and explain exactly what happened.

Sincerely yours,

Bette Davis

Dear Bette Davis:

Here is my problem: I am eighteen-years-old and am married, but I have been separated from my husband for four months. During this time I have been corresponding with a boy I knew and went with before I married. I am very much in love and he loves me also.

He doesn't know I am married and I haven't told him because he wants to get married on his furlough which will be soon.

I get a check from my husband every month and my mother depends on it. My husband is willing for me to get a divorce, but my mother is against it.

Should I get a divorce and marry Bill against my mother's will, or should I tell him I am married and call it off?

Charlene M.

Dear Mrs. M:

Under ordinary circumstances, I believe all of us should have respect for mothers and defer to their judgment.

However, in your case, I think your mother is grossly unfair and is behaving in a manner that may ruin three lives.

Unless your mother is an invalid, she should make some move to take care of herself and let you live a normal life, making your own decisions.

As for the boy with whom you are in love, it seems to me that when he comes home on furlough, you should tell him the whole truth. If he loves you as much as you say, he will be willing to wait for marriage until you can get this other situation cleared up!

Sincerely yours,

Bette Davis

Dear Miss Davis:

For six years I've lived and breathed Bette Davis—and everything connected with her. Lately I've had a brain storm. Although life isn't quite as exciting and fascinating as it could be. I don't think I'd have the courage to run away. But if I were ever invited any place by anyone—oh, happy day!

Since you receive so much pleasure in being president of committees, wouldn't you get even more pleasure out of sponsoring a club from which you could invite at least one member a year to Hollywood?

Gertrude L.

Dear Miss L:

As a matter of fact, I have long considered the possibility of bringing some new person with Stage appearance and screen ambitions to Hollywood each year.

However, I have now given up all hope of sponsoring this Hollywood trip for the duration. In the first place, the Government needs all available transportation space for essential war purposes. In the second place, Hollywood is now a very busy place and no one has time to devote to a guest.

But when the war is over, I hope to work something out along these lines.

Sincerely yours
Bette Davis

Dear Miss Davis:

From the time I was eight years old when I was picked by my teacher to speak a little piece about Lincoln, I wanted to be an actor. My father and mother tried to knock the idea out of my head and I was even forbidden to go to the movies, yet the more they tried to stop me, the more determined I was to continue. The family needed financial aid so I had to go to work and forget the idea of going to college. I consoled myself by attending the University Extension a few evenings a week and spending the other few with an amateur little theater group. After a few years I organized my own company and for six years have been turning out four or five plays a year.

Two years ago I fell in love with a very pretty girl and we were married. We now have a ten-week-old son who means everything in the world to us and for whom I want to work my fingers to the bone for. Anxious to do my part in helping our country, I applied for Volunteer Officer Candidate School but was turned down for lack of a college education and advised to stay with my family because of the boy's age and my wife's health. I have learned from the doctor that she will never be well again even though she is now up and around.

I've been debating with myself and toying with the idea of taking a chance in seeking employment in the studios next February if things don't change too harshly. I'm saving a little extra money to tide my family over until I can land a job. Perhaps I would have a chance in the stenographic department since I operate a stereotype at a rapid rate. Someday I might even get a chance to do "extra" work.

Please don't be angry with me for taking this liberty, but being the genuine person you are, I'm sure you'll see my point.

Roger K

Dear Mr. K:

I agree with you that you have a problem and it seems to me that you are approaching it in the right way. There is an old bromide, "Nothing ventured, nothing hath," which surely applies to your case.

You have been wise in saving up money enough to take care of your family obligations during your absence and I think you might as well take a chance in California. After all, it isn't as if you were coming out here with only the hope of getting into pictures immediately; you are a capable court reporter, so your secretarial work must be the best. Although you feel that this secretarial work has put you in a rut, it will stand you in good stead while you are getting acquainted with your new environment.

Considering your prolonged stage experience, your energy and ambition, who knows what might happen? The trip, I should think, would be worth trying

The best of luck to you.

Sincerely,

Bette Davis

Dear Miss Davis:

Just two weeks ago I met a very good- looking air cadet at a dance. Afterward I let him take me home. I asked him if he had a special girl at home or off somewhere and he said, "No," and asked me why.

I told him that I would like to hear from him when he went back to the "field." He said he would like to hear from me, too.

Well, he asked me what I was going to write him in my letters and I said. "What do you want me to say?"

He drew me up to him and kissed me. He asked me, "Now do you know what I want you to say in your letters?" Then he kissed me again.

Then he whispered to me that he loved me. He told me three or four times. How sweet I was.

Well, he got my address before he left and said he would write the very next day, but I have never received a letter, card, or anything from him. I don't suppose, now, that I ever will. Do you think I did or said something wrong? I love him. I know.

Miss Davis, boys just don't go around telling every girl they meet they love them. Or do they? Won't you please try to help me?

Yours truly,
Jane S.

Dear Miss S:

There is a verse from Shakespeare, "Much Ado About Nothing" that I think may fit your case:

"Sigh no more, ladies, sigh no more.
Men were deceivers ever,
One foot in sea, and one on shore,
To one thing constant never.
Then sigh not so, but let them go,

And be you blithe and bonny,
Converting all your sounds of woe
Into hey nonny, nonny."

Sincerely yours,
Bette Davis

Dear Bette Davis:

This letter will be full of nothing but trouble that I've had since I started with my love affairs.

I am greatly confused as I seem to be in love with two brothers and the two brothers seem to be in love with me. They quarrel over me; when I go out with one of them I am almost sure I love him best, but I get the same feeling when I go out with the other one.

The younger brother is more of the quiet type. If he sees me walking on the street, he'll only say as much as "hello." But when he goes out with me he shows me a great deal of love. The older brother pays attention to me regardless of where I am and acts a little more jokey than romantic, yet shows interest in me.

Please- write and tell me what I should do - depart from both of them, or what? I'm afraid I am causing trouble for both brothers.

Nancy Lou J.

Dear Miss J:

If, as you see, both brothers are in love with you, yet you cannot make up your mind between them, it would be better not to see either of them. This situation, as you say yourself, cannot but eventually cause enormous trouble between them.

However, I would judge that the brother you described as the "quiet" one is really in love with you. At any rate, he would make the better husband. It may be fun now with the brother who seems "more jokey than romantic," but over a long period of years this joking might wear rather thin. This type of man is apt not to confine his joking to you alone, but usually has fun with everyone he meets. Remember this in trying to solve your problem, because of course only you can solve it.

Bette Davis

Dear Miss Davis:

I have a very serious problem to face and I believe you can help me.

I have been married eighteen months and I have a baby boy eight-months-old. I had the baby because I thought a child would change my husband, but it hasn't. He still thinks he is single and wants to go out night after night, alone.

I don't believe in tying a man down, but I think I am entitled to a little freedom, such as going to the movies. My husband even objects to my taking a walk, wheeling the baby. When we have arguments about anything, no matter how small, he beats me unmercifully.

On his free day from the factory, he never stays at home but always goes out with other men. I have thought repeatedly of leaving him, but he threatens to take the baby if I do. At present I am only staying with him for the sake of the baby, but I don t think I can stand his abuse much longer.

My problem is this: Should I leave him and let him take the baby, or should I fight for my child? I think I would die if he took my baby away from me. Please advise me.

Mrs. T. W.

Dear Mrs W:

To begin with, I'm sure you will agree with me that a good marriage is worth preserving, only so long as it contributes to your dignity as a human being.

If your husband continues to behave like a single man, and if he continues to abuse you, you should certainly divorce him (or separate if your religion forbids divorce). When I suggest this drastic step, I assume that you are doing absolutely nothing to exasperate your husband, or to cause him to abuse you and leave you alone night after night.

You tell me that you are remaining with your husband and enduring his brutality only for the sake of your child. We all know that the most desirable environment for a child is one in which a normal home is maintained, presided over by a congenial father and mother. However, I am firmly convinced that enormous damage can be done to any child, no matter how young, when it is subjected to constant quarreling and contention between its parents. It may well ruin his or her life.

If you have witnesses who will testify to the manner in which you say your husband has been treating you, there should be nothing to hinder you getting custody of the baby. He certainly, as you describe him, is hardly a good father for any child. In making your decision, I feel that you should consider only the development and happiness of your son.

Bette Davis.

Dear Miss Davis:

I am taking the liberty of writing to you in the hope that you will be able to help me. Fear and worry are killing me. Twenty-three years ago I married a man of Mohammedan race. I have four girls and one son. We once owned a small home, but lost it through my husband's vice, who spent his nights away from home.

I raised my children myself and worked far into the night. When the children started school, my troubles began. They were taunted, blackguarded and asked. "What are you?" They said, "You aren't white and you aren't black. If you don't tell, we will beat you up after school."

Due to this constant picking, they have become nervous wrecks and fear has kept them friendless. They spend their time in the house and you might say we live in a world of our own. The youngest girl is sixteen, the next seventeen, the next nineteen. Then comes my son of twenty, and my oldest daughter, twenty-two. My son and oldest daughter support us as we haven't seen their father for twelve years.

It breaks my heart to see other young girls go out and enjoy themselves while my children never go anywhere. We have been advised to move into a small country town where we could have a garden and flowers, but I don't know where we could find such a place.

I am alone, unhappy, miserable woman. Dear Miss Davis, please write to me and tell me what is best to do for my children and myself, for I am afraid some kind of disaster is bound to happen to us as the situation is getting beyond our control.

Mrs. Hester F.

Dear Mrs. F:

You state that your fear for your children is killing you. Personally, I don't think you should censure yourself for the difficulties they find themselves in after twenty-three years. You must have been very much in love with your husband or you wouldn't have married him: therefore you have nothing of which to be ashamed. No one really understands the nature of love; it seems many times to spring up between two people of totally different races and creed, without explanation.

You have surely done well by your children to have taken care of them and brought them up without the help of a father in the later years. Now, you must allow your children to solve their own problems.

Fifty percent of solving any situation lies in first accepting the facts of the case, especially if there is absolutely nothing that can be done about changing those facts. Your children's father was Mohammedan, therefore they must, protect themselves, be proud of their race. If they adopt this attitude, it will be impossible for others to ridicule them. It seems to me that they should find out as much as possible about the history of the Mohammedans. Any public library will undoubtedly prove to be a treasure house of exciting information about the forebears of your husband's race. With so many American troops in Mohammedan countries, your children would soon find themselves in the midst of interesting discussion, I should think.

Frankly, I don't believe your children's situation can be solved by moving to another community. Your same problem would most likely exist everywhere you went. It is a situation that your children must solve right in their own home, by meeting it with courage and pride.

Bette Davis

Dear Madam:

I am twenty-years-old and in service. I had a hard time trying to convince a young lady to begin a love affair with me, but eventually I did. It has been for the space of six years since we began.

Since I have been with the chains of war bound around me, I don't hear from her. I have scrutinized my life to see if I can find a fault, but the only reason I can find is that I am working for Uncle Sam.

Perhaps she is discouraged with me because we can't walk in the park, or can't talk face-to-face or over the telephone as we used to do. May I look to you for advice?

James C.

Dear Sergeant C:

I suspect that the difficulty lies entirely with your being with Uncle Sam, a matter over which you have no control.

Your girl has probably been as lonely as you have been since you went away and I imagine she's extremely discouraged about not being able to see you more often. I imagine you just have to be patient with the non-progress of your love affair until you can see her again.

My only suggestion is - deluge her with letters. She will then know that you haven't forgotten her and that is automatically a help always.

Bette Davis

Dear Miss Davis:

I am a girl of eighteen years, have golden blonde hair, green eyes, fair complexion and a pug nose. I'm five feet and an a half inch, weight 100 pounds. I have a little girl who is one-year-old. I have no parents and my husband will soon be in service. The prospect is so lonely.

Miss Davis, would you help me? I want to be an actress or a dancer in the movies.

I have nobody out in California, so could you or would you let my baby and me come to you for a few weeks so I could have a chance? I'll even scrub your floors.

Toni L.

Dear Mrs. L:

To be lonely is one of the most tragic things in all the world, but the solution is not coming to live with me.

Your offer to scrub my floors is very generous, but I'm sure you can find something to do in the city in which you are living that would be far more interesting - and easier on your hands.

As to becoming an actress or a dancer in the movie - prove yourself on the stage first.

You will be able to overcome your loneliness, I'm sure, if you will keep busy at some war work.

Bette Davis

Dear Miss Davis:

I am a girl of sixteen. Last summer I was sick and lost all my hair. I would like to know if you could get me a wig. The color of my hair was dark brown, my face is oval shape and my head is the size of Virginia Weidler's. I would be glad to pay any expense.

Jean B.

Dear Miss B:

I suggest that you write to Mr. Pere Westmore in care of Warner Brothers Studios, Burbank, California.

Give him your complete head measurements and the color of hair desired. Also, supply him with a picture of yourself, taken before you lost your hair. In this way he will be able to design an appropriate hair-dress for your type of face.

If you do not hear from Mr. Westmore, please let me know.

Bette Davis

Dear Mrs. Farnsworth:

I've been married almost six years to a man thirteen years my senior. We are very much in love and I am happier today than I was when I married.

I read in a movie magazine where a star's standing was judged by his "fan" mail. So I wrote a "fan" letter to Dennis Morgan, wanting to do my part toward boosting him to success. As an answer, the studio sent me his photograph.

My in-laws were at my house the day it arrived. Then the ribbing really started and several days later they brought me a clipping about "females" making fools of themselves over male stars.

I want to know if you think I did right or wrong. Don't you think it possible for the average 'movie-goer' like me to be interested in a male movie star because she likes his work and wants to help him to success?

Mrs. J. M.

Dear Mrs. M:

All I can say is that when "females," as your in-laws call us, stop "making fools" of ourselves over actors - again your in-laws' idea or actors will most certainly be in the soup.

The value of Dennis Morgan, or that of any other actor, is judged by his studio according to the number of people who go to see his pictures and how many of those people write and tell him so.

Mr. Morgan sent you his picture, I'm sure, so that you would know how much he appreciated the boost you were giving his career, and those who put any other interpretation on it do not understand the importance of fan mail in Hollywood.

Believe me, all of us on the screen are grateful to people like you who write us.

Bette Davis

Dear Miss Davis:

Within a short time I am going to make my debut in the opera, 'La Traviata,' in which I will sing Violetta.

Because of financial reasons, my gowns for the opera are proving more expensive than I can afford.

During one of the scenes in "Now, Voyager," you wore a sequin cape which would be an ideal costume for the first act entrance. I was wondering if you might allow me to borrow it.

Martha M.

Dear Miss M:

I inquired at the wardrobe department about the sequin cape, only to learn it will be impossible to loan it to you.

The war has affected the studios quite as much as it has other industries. As you know, there are many materials no longer available, so the studio must conserve those they have. There is now a strict rule in the wardrobe department that nothing is to be loaned under any circumstance. I tried a mild sort of wheedling, without any result. I am so sorry.

My best wishes for your success,

Bette Davis

Dear Miss Davis:

I should like to employ an agent, but there are some things I should know about agents first, I think.

How does one go about employing an agent? In general, what are agents' fees for beginners? What service does an agent render?

Alice Z.

Dear Miss Z:

Employing an agent usually comes about in this way: Some agent becomes interested in your career and seeks to sign you as a client. It is then your prerogative to hire him or to look around for someone who, you feel, could do a better job for you. At this point one thing for you to consider very seriously is securing an agent who is truly interested in you and in advancing your career.

I believe the law allows an agent ten percent of your salary.

An agent's duties resolve themselves into the complete management of your career. He advises and guides you in a million different ways. He assists you in straightening out contractual difficulties, helps you in the choice of scripts and arranges your personal appearance and your work on the radio.

If an agent does not help you with all these things, he is not being fair with you and so is not worthy of your employ.

Bette Davis

My dear Miss Davis:

Unlike many girls I know, I do not wish to become a movie actress. My ambition was to become a model, but nature has seen to it that I'll never have a career of that sort.

I am still in my teens, but out of high school. I am just too tall: five-feet-eleven inches. Crowding six feet as you can see. I weigh 150, but everyone tells me that I am proportioned excellently.

On the whole, though. I feel very conspicuous at all times. This is not intended for a "sob story" so please don't accept it as such. I'm going to try to build some kind of career, but heavens only knows what it shall be. Could you advise?

Zora W.

Dear Miss W:

Height has little to do with a girl's beauty. Pride of courage and grace of movement are real determining factors.

I have talked to several persons about careers for tall girls and I have learned that in Earl Carroll's famous club in Hollywood there are two girls who are an even six feet tall.

At Paramount Studios, Ginger Rogers is currently working in a picture called "Lady In The Dark" and in the dream sequence a chorus of fashion models is used to create a superb effect. Every girl in that sequence is six feet in heels.

So I don't believe height should deter you from seeking any career that appeals to you, particularly that of a model. You should be ideal for this work.

Bette Davis

Dear Miss Davis:

I am a girl of seventeen. I have been married for almost five months. After the second month of my marriage, I knew I didn't love my husband, but he loves me so much that he said if I ever left him or anything happened to me, he would kill himself. He's just the sort who would, too.

He is extremely good to me and forever paying me compliments, but I just can't love him although I've tried very hard to make him a good wife.

He is an officer in the Army, the infantry, and he doesn't know how long he will be in The States.

Should I tell him now that I don't love him and leave, or should I somehow stick and try to make him happy while he is here?

Mrs D. M.

Dear Mrs M:

Apparently yours was a wartime marriage entered into without enough consideration. Since you are only seventeen, you should have waited to marry someone you were sure you would stay in love with longer than two months. You most certainly shouldn't continue to live with a man whom you can't love - that would be extremely dishonest. The only thing to do, it seems to me, is for you to tell your husband how you now feel about him. Perhaps, since he's very likely older than you, he will understand. The fact that he may not be in this country much longer is one more reason for your coming to some conclusion at once. It would be grossly unfair for you to let him go on thinking when he returned, you would still be in love with him.

Yours sincerely

Bette Davis

Dear Miss Davis:

I'm not much for writing letters to other people for advice, but I thought maybe you could help me with this very difficult problem.

I am twenty-years-old and have a sister who's seventeen. My parents died only a few years ago and I have been supporting my sister and myself although she helps by taking care of children.

This is the trouble: She imagines herself to be in love with John Payne.

She has our rooms full of pictures of him until I can't bear the sight of his face. She has covered all our relatives' pictures with a picture of him. She never misses a movie he is in and lately has been spending everything she earns on magazines in which there is a picture of him.

I find her sitting in front of a mirror acting as if he were there. She pretends she is his girlfriend and even his wife. She doesn't go out with any other boys—she just moons over him.

I thought she would get over it, but it has gone on for over a year now.

Can you tell me what I can do to end this silly infatuation? I've tried taking her to see other stars, but she still holds on to him.

Yours in disgust.

Jeanne W.

Dear Miss W:

You have signed yourself , "yours in disgust," and I think perhaps that this is the whole trouble. It is possible your ridicule of your sister's devotion for Mr. Payne only incites her further, out of stubbornness. It is a well-known fact that when brothers or sisters disapprove of certain situations, the person in question is likely to cling to his or her ideal with twice the original determination.

There is a far better way of handling a situation of this kind. How well I remember how my own mother handled such things! When she disapproved of a beau, she was cordial towards him. She always made him welcome to our home - insisted, in fact, that I see him. It always worked; I recovered from my infatuation with the most amazing rapidity.

Why don't you try the same method? If this situation really worries you, why not rave about Mr. Payne even more than she does and pin up twice as many pictures? This shouldn't be much of a trial as Mr. Payne is a very attractive man.

It is certainly not unusual for your sister to admire more a man of Mr. Payne's caliber, who is remote from her, than a boy she could see all the time. Her admiration of Mr. Payne will probably make her a catch for any beau she eventually chooses.

Sincerely,

Bette Davis

Dear Miss Davis:

I am sixteen years of age and a sophomore in high school.

Here is my problem: I have superfluous hair on my face, hands and arms. If my face wasn't involved, I don't think I'd worry, but it seems everyone is just staring at me all the time. This makes me self-conscious. I am considered nice-looking, but not pretty.

I go out with a boy once in a while but it seems to me that no boy could ever fall in love with a girl who has a problem like mine.

Can you help me?

Altona M.

Dear Miss M:

I agree with you that you do have a problem. I chose your letter to answer because it dealt with a dilemma about which a great many girls have written to me.

I am told by those who should know that superfluous hair is something caused by a slightly physical disorder. This being the key, you should have a talk with your family doctor and I am certain he will be able to give you the assistance you need.

Don't worry about your future success with boys. Since you have started at sixteen to solve your problem by seeking medical advice, your popularity should not suffer in the least.

Sincerely,

Bette Davis

Dear Miss Davis:

I am twenty-two years of age and I am married to an Army officer who is going overseas in two months. I am going to have a baby next July and after the birth of my baby I want to work again. Before I was married I was a secretary and I want to continue doing that kind of work.

I have always wanted to live in Hollywood and do

stenographic work, but first I want to know if there are many girls out in Hollywood in search of stenographic work, as there are a lot of them trying to get into the movies. I definitely have no desire for acting, as I'm not the least bit talented, but I would be very happy working in a studio or for a movie star.

Of course, I will have my baby and enough money to live on even if I do not work. It will be a year before I decide to go out to Hollywood but I would like to know what you think my chances will be. Incidentally, I am considered a good stenographer. I can always go back to the company I previously worked for.

Do you think it would be wise for me to move to Hollywood in search of work? Will you please tell me what my chances would be?

Mrs. E. C.

Dear Miss C:

When you are well enough to go back to work, I would advise you to return to the company by which you were previously at.

Day after today I receive literally dozens of letters from all over the United States and Canada, from those who are eager to come to Hollywood to be artists, songwriters, secretaries, hairdressers in the studio and any one of dozens of other things.

Large as the motion-picture industry is, it still isn't vast enough to employ all those who, apparently, would like to engage in picture-making ,in any one of its phases. This means that most of those who come to Hollywood to find work are going to end by doing the type of work they left originally.

There will be one great difference, however. In the old environment, the workers had many friends. Girls had beaux whose family connections they knew. There was an established, pleasant routine in life - the lakes in summer, the League formal in winter, Bridge parties, church affairs, the life of a familiar community gave them a sense of belonging and well-being.

When one transplants to Hollywood, all those things are lost. Hollywood can be one of the loneliest spots on the face of the map. And its glamour is a thing that exists only at private gatherings about which the newcomer will hear nothing much, much less attend.

For those girls who would like to do secretarial work in a studio or for a star, I can only say that this sort of work is highly technical. It requires years of preparation - of a special sort.

Sincerely yours,

Bette Davis

Dear Miss Davis:

I am twenty-one years old. I am desperately in love with a man fifteen years my senior. He, however, is married to a woman who is hopelessly insane.

There is no hope of our marrying, even though the law decrees that in a few years he is entitled to a divorce. He says he cannot bring himself to completely desert this helpless woman.

We have been living together for one year and have been ideally happy! But now my sins have caught up with me. I am to bear his child in seven months I haven't told him yet, but I can't keep this secret very much longer. I am desperately frightened.

Isabell W.

Dear Miss W:

You must tell the man with whom you are in love, the truth about your condition at once. This problem is certainly not yours to bear alone, but both of your responsibilities.

My heart goes out to you because, as you say, your situation is desperate.

I am sure, since you have been so happy together, he will find some solution to your problem.

Sincerely,

Dear Miss Davis:

I am nineteen, and a junior at the university I am studying pre-med and intend to become a doctor. Last year, while I was taking my nurse's aide course, I met one of the interns in the hospital and we have become staunch friends. He is American, but his parents were Japanese. He is twenty-six and is already on his way to becoming an outstanding surgeon.

About a month ago he told me he loved me and wanted to marry me, but that he loved me too much to ask me to sacrifice my entire life for him. I love him very dearly—really love him It is not pity, which it might have been (because some people have treated him very unkindly since the war). He has been trying desperately to get into the Army but, because of a few technicalities, he cannot. This has made him very unhappy.

We are both Catholic, so there would be no religious difficulty. My mother, my father and my brother all say that if I really love him and cannot be happy without him. I should marry him. If we should marry, I would continue my studies and so would he.

Since this is something which concerns our whole lives I feel I should definitely have advice.

Kathryn L.

Dear Miss L:

I would say that, since you love this man and you seem to have considered all the difficulties involved very carefully, you should marry him.

However, as you yourself have stated, there will be problems of many sorts. The unkindness you say some people have shown him must be expected at the present time. Even after the war's over there may be bitterness in some minds.

However, since you will both be following a learned profession, your friends will be derived from the same intellectual sphere. Doctors, lawyers, writers, artists, have a strong tendency to accept a person upon merit and not to discriminate against him because of racial accident of birth.*

There is one thing I do think you should pay special attention to before making your decision: The question of children. You have the right to choose your own life and the intellect to make it a happy one, but - and remember, please, that this is entirely a personal opinion - I feel that you have no right to bring children into a situation with which they might never be able to cope.*

Sincerely yours
Bette Davis

Dear Mrs. Farnsworth:

I have been married five years, have two lovely children and a husband, and a swell home. And yet I am unhappy.

My husband and I were both born and bred in New York City and after we were married he was transferred over 400 miles away from all our folks and friends.

I have tried to make other friends and to find interests that will keep me busy and stop thinking and longing for New York, but it's no go. I'm getting nervous, thin, and there is no improvement as the years go by. You never make real friends when you reach thirty.

I know I could persuade my husband to give up his present position, but he'd have to work for half the salary he's now getting. His position here is a lifetime one. He has tried without success for a transfer, so it's either give up this spot and work for a small salary and be rich in friends and our folks—or a larger salary with a nice home and no one ever ringing our bell.

What would you do, Miss Davis?
Marcella Z.

Dear Mrs. Z:

In this situation, it seems to me, your husband is the most to be considered. Wouldn't it be extremely unfair to force him to give up a "lifetime" position, as you describe it, at a comfortable salary, and return to a tedious, underpaid job, just because you like New York better?

I really can't agree with you when you say that one never makes real friends when one reaches thirty. It is true that one may not make exactly the same type of friends that one knew in their younger days, but many warm and lasting acquaintances can be cultivated in the mature years.

Perhaps your trouble is that you are thinking too much of yourself and your discontent. In these days when there is so much real tragedy in the world, it behooves all of us to put aside self-pity. You should take an active part in the life of your community.

In every town there are Red Cross Chapters with a crying need for volunteers: there are nutrition classes to be attended and study clubs to be joined.

The moment you put your past life in the background - and stop thinking about New York - and the moment you begin to take an honest interest in your present surroundings and the people you meet, you won't have to worry about that non-ringing doorbell. You may even have to muffle it to get some rest!

Sincerely,
Bette Davis

Dear Miss Davis:

I am seventeen years old. About two months ago I met a very nice boy of twenty-three. We began to go out together and found our friendship turning into something deeper. My mother and father like this boy very much.

Now something has come up to spoil everything. One of the friends of the fellow told me that he was married! I simply couldn't believe it at first, but the next evening when he came over I asked him for the truth. It made him simply furious at me. He said he was married: that when he met me he hadn't dreamed he would get to care for me.

That happened about a week ago and since that time I have heard from him just once. He asked me to go to a movie and I went because I hadn't told my parents the truth about him, so they would have asked questions if I had refused. On the way home he said he couldn't keep away from me and that he was going to fix matters so that we could be together always. That should have made me happy, but it didn't. I'm all mixed up inside. What do you think I should do?

Gretchen J.

Dear Miss J:

You should tell your parents the truth about the boy and I think they will agree with me that you should not see him again. Under the existing circumstances nothing but unhappiness for all three of you (the boy's wife included) can possibly come of such a situation.

He had no reason to be "simply furious" with you, as he has no right whatsoever to interfere with your life, nor to jeopardize your future happiness.

Yours sincerely,
Bette Davis

Dear Miss Davis:

I am a girl of seventeen and I have a boyfriend overseas whom I love very much. As I am Canadian, I wish to join the Air Force—I am eligible—but he won't hear of it. He says he is fighting so we girls won't have to. He also doesn't think it is a girl's place to join up and be put in uniform.

He says that if I do join up, he will have nothing to do with me. Now, Miss Davis, I would like to know what you would do in my place: Join up and fight for the love of my country, or stay at home and wait for him to return, as he wishes.

Carol D.

Dear Miss D:

If joining the Air Force is something that you sincerely wanted, if you honestly feel it will contribute towards winning the war more quickly, you must do it. You have to live with yourself; you must behave in accordance with your convictions.

As for your beau, he must realize how much we need every person to do what they can. The time has passed when women must simply sit at home and wait for a soldier's return, without doing anything constructive. What would other allied nations have done if their women hadn't contributed to the war effort as well as the men?

It seems to me that you must do what you feel is right in this situation and in the long run I'm sure your beau will understand.

Bette Davis

Dear Miss Davis:

I'm sure you will be able to help me. My problem seems to be confronting many people. How does one overcome self-consciousness and stage fright?

Some day I want to be a high-school music teacher and a radio singer. I am said to play the piano well and people say I have a very sweet coloratura voice. But when I play the piano at concerts, my legs give way and I shake to the marrow of my bones. I can't get up in school and make a simple five-minute speech without my voice developing a tremor.

I do wish you could give me some firsthand information on how to overcome these embarrassing emotions. Thank you.

Donna M.

Dear Miss M:

Stage fright is a very usual disease among performers. There is no complete cure for it. As a matter of fact, it turns out to be usually your friend and not your enemy.

You will find, I'm sure, that as your technique improves and as you gain confidence in yourself as a performer, your nervousness will subside so there will be no visible sign of it to your audience. The best way to improve your technique is to study and to make as many appearances as possible before an audience. These two things will increase your confidence in yourself.

But I never wish to lose your stage fright completely. That is what keeps you up to doing your best. Good luck!

Bette Davis

Dear Miss Davis:

While sitting in my room on this lonely Sunday afternoon, I happened to pick up a Photoplay Magazine. I read an article where a mother was pleading for her child to have the proper training for a career.

There seem to be many people who are asking for your help. I heartily disagree with them. I can well remember how I used to write to Hollywood people, pleading for their help. Now, I can see how wrong I was because there are thousands of people asking for help and it is impossible for stars to render universal aid.

Miss Davis, I am solving my own problem. Instead of waiting for someone to give me my chance I decided to work things out for myself. This is how: People have raved about my singing since I was fifteen-years-old. I graduated from high school at seventeen. I did not see a possible chance for continuing my education so I worked and paid for voice lessons, piano, dramatics and harmony.

I am now twenty and have won a scholarship in music. My former voice teacher was so proud of me that she is buying all my textbooks. I work off campus for my room and board.

I may add that I am a Negro girl, so life is a little more difficult for me than for a white girl. I have written this letter because I wanted to ask if you don't agree that a person who has will power and determination will win. Movie stars have had to struggle to get what they have today, so why can't the ordinary, unknown person do the same?

Willa Jean T.

Dear Miss T:

Thank you for your very charming letter. I certainly agree with you that a person with will power and determination usually gets what he wants; the life stories of most successful people will prove that they have had plenty of struggle along the way. As the old saying goes, God helps those who help themselves.

Bette Davis

Dear Miss Davis:

I am writing to ask your advice, being that you are modern and not a narrow-minded, prejudiced person.

As there is a shortage of boys, my girlfriends and I have been going to various dances and roller-skating rinks where we meet various types of service men, mainly sailors.

Naturally, after the dance or skating party, we go out to cat with them and then they escort us home. My mother doesn't mind because she knows I have always confided in her and wouldn't do anything wrong.

But the women on the block been seeing me come home with them and have been talking. Some past friends say I should not do that as sailors have a bad reputation and all that stuff.

I say if a girl is good, then the fellow behaves. Is this proper or should I, because of the neighbors, discontinue having them take me home?

Madeline J.

Dear Miss J:

I should think the days of being prejudiced against service men would have passed.

I, through my work at the Canteen, have seldom come in contact with finer boys. The day of the "girls in every port" for a sailor has now become just a very stale joke.

If you are a person who minds her own business, you have a right to expect the same attitude from others. Most certainly you and your mother are the best possible judges of the way you are managing your lives. It is nobody's business but yours. So don't let yourself be upset by what is really only petty gossip.

Bette Davis

Dear Miss Davis:

I am a girl of nineteen, married, and have a two-year-old son. My husband is twenty-one. We have been married for three years and love each other very much, but our tastes are not just alike in all things. For instance, I am more settled than he. I like good clean fun, sports such as bowling, swimming and so forth.

Although neither of us dances, he thinks we should learn so I suggested we learn to dance at home with some of our friends. He doesn't think that would be fun, yet I don't approve of "juke joints"—so we are out of agreement there. I think it would be better for us to stay at home since we have no one to care for our son.

I think he should be more serious- minded and be thinking of saving money for the future. We have had two bitter quarrels and he thinks there is no happiness for us together, but I think there is. I'm fighting against a divorce because of the baby and our love for each other. He and the baby are crazy about each other.

My parents want me to divorce him. Would you please tell me how I can make my husband happy and still remain decent in the eyes of our friends?

Mrs. M.

Dear Mrs. M:

Although you are careful, in your letter, to reiterate how much you and your husband love each other, it may be perhaps that the love is more on your side than on that of your husband. You seem much more mature for your years than he does.

There is one truth that all women have to face, it seems to me, and that is: There is nothing more heartbreaking than trying to force a man to pretend a love and loyalty he no longer feels. If, however, you can honestly say to yourself that your husband still loves you, then anything you may do to preserve your marriage will be worth it.

If not, the problem before you is probably that of giving up gracefully and building a new life for yourself, but that is a decision that only you can make.

Bette Davis

Dear Miss Davis:

I would like some advice from you. I am in high school where I am called better than an average student. I am tall (five-foot-seven inches) and not so beautiful, and I am just about always in the "doghouse."

Here is my trouble. I sing—my voice has been trained by my mother who sang on the radio and by the best music teachers that can be had. I also act and I am told that I do okay. My mother wants me to be a singer because my voice is high and powerful, but I don't want to be a singer. And I don't want to be on the stage or in the movies.

I am happy only when I am working with chemicals up at the University where I am taking chemical warfare and I hope soon to go to work in the arsenal. Mother has told me I am to go to a music school on the East Coast.

How am I to tell her I do not want to go? I suppose I should go since all this money has been spent on lessons, but I know that if I go I will never be really happy again.

Anne J.

Dear Miss J:

I think we all find our mothers to be very understanding people. You, of course, must tell your mother how you feel about a singing career and what your ambitions really are.

This is the kind of thing that must be weighed in the balance very carefully, since what you decide now will affect the whole future course of your life.

If you have a real talent, it would be a crime to ignore it.

Talk this over with your mother and listen to her carefully. You are still very young; perhaps you will find that your mother's idea will be very advantageous for you.

Bette Davis

Dear Miss Davis:

I am twenty-seven, married and the mother of two lovely little boys. I can't say honestly that I was ever madly in love with my husband. I married him because all my girlfriends were being married; because I wasn't interested in anyone else, because he was ambitious and nice-looking. Not very solid reasons on which to build a life, I'm afraid. Yet, I suspect that my case isn't too far from that of my many goals.

A year ago an insurance salesman came to my door to ask about renewing some of my husband's policies. I invited the man in—as my husband was due home in ten minutes —and we chatted conventionally. Suddenly he strolled over to the bookcase and picked out a volume, then another. We began to talk literature, one of my true passions.

My husband was late that night—of all nights—but when he finally arrived. I felt as if I had known this man always. A week later he brought back the policies in the morning. He remained for luncheon and stayed all afternoon, while we played symphonies on the recorder and talked.

I knew I was desperately in love with him, but I knew there wasn't anything to be done about it.

One night I left the children with my sister and this man and I took a long drive into the country. As we turned off the main highway, we saw what looked like a body at the side of the road. We parked and he went back to investigate. Without touching the poor crushed thing, he found that it was an aged man who might have been struck by a hit and run driver.

He came back and we talked it over. We decided not to report it—because of the circumstances. We talked amongst ourselves and decided it was hopeless. He decided to join the Army— and he left the next day.

Meanwhile, this is what happened: During the time we

were parked in the grove, one of the local high-school boys I passed on the highway, saw the body and got out to investigate. He must have been driving rather fast, because there were skid marks on the pavement. He had been stopped only a few seconds (according to his story) when one of the town officials, a blue-nosed, miserly, cantankerous old reprobate —drove up. He accused the boy of having killed the itinerant.

Since the boy is a minor and since the evidence against him was entirely circumstantial, he has been placed on probation. He has protested his innocence forty ways, but you know what he's up against.

Now, here is the thing that is bothering me: I know positively that the boy is innocent because of the time involved. I know that we should have reported what we found at once— and we could have spared the boy and his family all the misery they have endured. This thing, this injustice, may embitter him and affect his entire future.

But what about me? The man is gone and I don't hear from him by mail. If I do come forward and substantiate the boy's story, I'm going to be our town's scarlet woman. No one would believe that our trip to the grove was innocent. Speaking up may easily cost me my husband, my children and my honored placed in our community.

What would you do, Miss Davis?

Johanna H.

Dear Mrs. H:

Unfortunately there is nothing in the world for you to do but to go to the authorities and substantiate the boy's story. You are quite right in saying that this injustice may ruin his life; should he – out of a spirit of defiance and bravado – get into further trouble, you would never forgive yourself.

As for yourself, things may be made very difficult for you. However, you will find that along with those who condemn you, will be those who will admire you for the courage telling your story is going to require. You may lose some friends, but those you keep and those you gain will repay you.

You must go to your husband first and tell the truth. You may find that he will believe you implicitly and be a bulwark of strength for you. But that is a chance you must take.

The future of that boy must be your first consideration.

Bette Davis

Dear Miss Davis:

I need advice badly. I am a high-school girl of seventeen, very independent, and rather sure of my abilities. I have a wonderful home, lovely clothes and devoted parents yet I am missing some fun that every girl takes for granted.

I have been brought up to respect my parents' judgment, obey their wishes and act according to the rules of well-bred young ladies. My problem, Miss Davis, is shyness. I am very self-conscious and unsure of myself in public.

As I have said, I am sure of my school studies. I will graduate with highest honors in 1943, yet when I meet people I become uneasy, fussed and miserable. I have never been able to make friends easily.

I am five-feet-four-inches tall, I have an off-shade of blonde hair, hazel eyes, a good complexion and a desire to be sophisticated and grownup. I have one flaw in my appearance, that is overweight. I weigh twenty pounds more than I should so my clothes don't look well on me.

Next fall my parents want to send me to college. I'm afraid to go, as I can't make friends. I am scared to death of becoming homesick and thoroughly disliking school.

In closing I want to add that being heavy makes me feel out of place and unnecessary with girls my own age.

Miss Davis, can you help? If you find time to answer my letter I promise faithfully to follow your instructions and I'll let you know the results. Thank you again.

Thelma T.

Dear Miss T:

The first thing for you to remember is that the girls of seventeen are often plump. This is called "baby fat" and it doesn't mean that overweight is going to be a permanent thing. It is very hard for me to tell from your letter whether you are a hearty eater, or whether you have ever done anything to try to lose weight. If your excess pounds are making you unhappy, as they seem to be, why don't you consult your family doctor? Being overweight can be the result of many different things, but sometimes it is glandular and can be quite easily remedied.

Whatever you do, don't select a diet from a magazine and follow it without consulting your doctor. And don't be afraid that diet consists only of lettuce and carrots. Nowadays many delicious things are included in all diets.

I do know that overweight does make one self-conscious. When you have corrected the problem, I think everything else will smooth out and you will really look forward to college. Do let me know how you get along.

Sincerely,

Bette Davis

Dear Miss Davis:

This is the first time I have ever written a letter to a person I don't know, but I'm so discouraged that I'm ready to try anything once. I saw the article in Photoplay and decided to write.

I'm seventeen years of age and never had a date. All my girlfriends have had dates, but not me. It isn't that I mind so much because I go to school and after school I work. I go roller-skating every Sunday and not one boy skates with me. I feel so cheap sometimes that I feel like crying. I guess I'm about the only girl sitting down when it's skating time for couples only.

I'm not very pretty. Just about average. All my friends tell me it is because I'm so short. That's true. I'm only four-feet-eight and a half inches high. Maybe that's why, but there are a lot of small boys, too.

I want to know why the boys won't skate with me. I'm sure that I haven't got B.O. because I'm a very neat person and think of all these possibilities. Won't you please advise me on what to do?

Yours,
Maybelle M.

Dear Miss M:

After reading your letter, I have the feeling that you, personally, suspect why you are not popular. Being popular at seventeen is not everything in the world: still it does mean a great deal. I know.

I wish you would write me a more detailed letter, telling me more about yourself and your life in general. The brevity of your letter makes it difficult for me to know what to suggest.

Sincerely,
Bette Davis

Dear Miss Davis:

I have just finished reading your very interesting article in Photoplay-Movie Mirror. I have the bright idea that you may be able to help me also, along with the millions of other discontented women and girls in America.

I am engaged to a boy in the U. S Army whom I have known for three years. My problem is just a simple one to many people, but to me it seems a tragedy: I chew my fingernails.

I have done this ever since I can remember, I have tried everything. I have even tried medicine which I have applied freely, but all to no avail for I just keep on biting my nails.

Miss Davis, my fiancé is coming home in March and he hates my nails as they are. Can you, and will you try to help me? I will deeply appreciate any suggestion you can make.

Rosemary W.

Dear Miss W:

Nail-biting is a tragedy and extremely difficult to cure oneself of. I know because I chewed my nails once to the destruction of my entire family and circle of friends. My mother used all the medicines recommended and tried every other known remedy without any result.

I found out that what cured myself of this habit was like everything else; it's not a question of medicine or fancy tricks, it is simply a matter of your own determination and some incentive helps. You see, my first beau was so disgusted with the appearance of my hands - that I, because I wanted to be perfect to him - just stopped!

Think how happy your fiancé will be if he knows you love him enough to be able to stop biting your nails. He will know what a battle it was and love you all the more for it. And think how proud you'll be of yourself, and of your strength of will power. I am sure you can do it!

People have lost fiancé's for smaller reasons than this. Had you ever thought of it that way?

Sincerely,

Bette Davis

Dear Miss Davis:

I'm a colored girl of sixteen. Of course, I lead the normal life of any teen-age girl except that I have quite a few problems. The first is clothes. The greatest problem is color that will be becoming to me. My complexion is a light brown- olive shade. Could you please tell me what colors I could wear most flatteringly?

The second problem is my skin. It is good except for blackheads. I was told that soap and water are most important factors and I cleanse my face frequently, but the blackheads persist.

I can't end this letter without telling you that I think you're perfectly "solid" and I'm really looking forward to an answer to my letter.

Sincerely,

Theresa K

Dear Miss K:

It seems to me that the colors you should avoid are green, brown, navy blue, and black. You should be able to wear red, yellow, chalk white, turquoise and royal blue to advantages.

As for your skin, I'm not quite sure what you mean by "I cleanse my face frequently." The only way to obtain a really clean skin is to cleanse it thoroughly twice a day.

Sincerely,

Bette Davis

Dear Miss Davis:

I have just finished reading your advice to other girls who have problems and decided that you were the one to help me, if you will.

I just came from high school in a small town, to a big city, where I am working. While I was in a small town, I went with a boy fairly steadily although I did go out with other boys, too. He is in the Air Force now and is still as crazy about me as he always was. However, I have never loved him, although I think he is a fine chap.

I am sixteen and all my friends are either engaged or about to be married. I feel that I should become engaged, with the war on and all.

However, I haven't met anyone I do love and I am beginning to despair that maybe I never will.

Please let me tell you a few things about me. I come from a nice family, fairly well off, and they provide a good home. I have a good position and a lovely place to live, with friends, here in the city. I am five-feet-two, blonde and have a fair figure. I have attractive clothes; I sing and play the piano, love to dance and take part in all sports, especially tennis, golf and skiing. Being popular at home has spoiled me for being a social flop in the city. Although I have found oodles of new girl friends, the boys here just don't care for me.

I would appreciate it so much if you would tell me what to do about the boy I was telling you about and also what is wrong with me in my new environment. I feel so depressed, and I don't want to bother Mother and Dad.

Yours truly,
Alice B.

Dear Miss B:

Whether or not you are actually unpopular with the boys in your new home is impossible for me to judge. In everyone's life, you know, there are lulls; not every period in our lives can be equally exciting. Also, when anyone comes to a new city, one is apt to be more sensitive to the reactions of those about than normally. Just remember that you probably seem as strange to them as they do to you.

However, my general impression of your problem is that you are looking too hard for either a fiancé or a husband. I certainly don't believe you should be engaged to the boy in the Air Force if you do not love him.

Have you given much thought to the possibilities that some of the difference in your position now and in former years is due to the war? As you are living in a Canadian city, there are obviously few eligible men around and those who are available or busy trying to help win the war.

Perhaps I am wrong, but it has occurred to me - reading between the lines of your letter - that there may be one boy in particular whom you like and who is not very interested in you. Perhaps you are telling yourself that you are unpopular in general, simply as a defense mechanism.

When you say that you don't want to bother your father and mother with your problems, I can't agree with you. I believe you should talk this over with them, as they are more interested in you than anyone else in the world and they are certainly more qualified than anyone to give you advice in this matter.

Yours sincerely,

Bette Davis

Dear Miss Davis:

I have noticed in most of the motion pictures I have seen that the star's hair is so lustrous. I have tried everything known to mankind to achieve this, but alas! I brush my hair every night and wash it every other week with the best of shampoos. My hair is between blonde and brown and a difficult color to match.

What should I do to improve my hair?

Yours sincerely,

Adele D.

Dear Miss D:

Why shouldn't hair in motion pictures look lustrous and lovely? For instance, while I am making a picture, Margaret Donovan, my hairdresser, washes my hair every other day. However, you should see some of us between pictures!

One thing you can do to improve the sheen of your hair is to wash it more often than every other week. I think it should be washed once or twice a week. It is not necessary to go to a beauty shop, as this would be too expensive for most of us. You can learn to wash it yourself, at home.

Also, strange as it may seem, all shampoos are beneficial if your hair is oily (I checked with Miss Donovan.) I hope this will prove helpful to you.

Yours sincerely,

Bette Davis

Dear Miss Davis:

I wish you could help me, but I am afraid that I can't tell you clearly enough what my trouble is for you to give an answer to my problem.

I'm not bad-looking—a little too thin. Five-feet-eight and one-half inches tall and weigh 120 pounds. When I go out, I know I look as well as other girls whose hair is sometimes messy and whose clothes are sloppy. I am always neat, yet they will be laughing and happy and with a crowd and I will be alone.

I can always make conversation and I think I try to make it interesting, I say original things, yet nothing is ever appreciated. Everyone is always saying how- clever or pretty or this or that, some person is, yet they pass up all my good points. I want friends of my own age. The few I do have are at least fifteen years older than I. I am twenty-five. I want girls around to laugh and play and be silly once in a while instead of talking about such prosaic things as recipes, money matters, husband trouble—and absent members.

I collect records of popular orchestra and make scrapbooks of bands. I would like to be able to talk bands or movies with someone. I also like to read classics as well as best-sellers.

My husband doesn't help any as he is very quiet and doesn't dance although, for my sake, he is now taking lessons. We have been married three years and I guess we will always be married. He is eleven years older than I and is good to me, but I want friends and laughter, happiness and good times. Sometimes I try to explain it to my husband, but he says, "Don't I give you everything you want?"

I try to explain that it isn't money. It is just companionship. Walks in the fresh air, laughter and music, sharing good books, planning homey things together.

Miss Davis, should I wake up? Am I asleep? Am I

groping for things that can't happen to girls like me? Is it true, as people tell me, that women have very few friends? Oh, please let me know some way to change myself so that I can have friends.

Thank you for everything,
Zelma T.

Dear Miss T:

At the risk of being brutally frank, I must say that I think you are reading too many books and that you are living in a sort of dream world.

In, "Old Acquaintance," the picture in which I am working at present, the character of Millie is this sort of person.

It seems to me that you will make yourself a very unhappy person if you don't start to count your personal blessings. After all, no one has everything. As a matter of fact, there are a good many people in the world whom I would choose to be in preference to myself. As far as that goes, I don't think I have ever met a completely happy person.

However, those who live successfully are those who take stock of themselves and make the best of what they have. Such people bring joy to those around them - which in turn makes them happy.

Your desire to have friends is paramount with everyone. I am sure you'll find that, if you start making those around you happy, friends will flock to you. In these times, particularly, we have such millions of things to be thankful for - we, Americans! We should radiate good fortune to all we meet!

Sincerely,
Bette Davis

Dear Miss Davis:

I am seventeen-years-old and attend a private girl's boarding school. Five months ago I fell in love with a married doctor about the age of thirty-nine. I didn't fall in love with him at first sight—it took quite a while—but I've been in love with him ever since.

My parents know I have a crush on him and say nothing although they kid me once in a while for they think it's another puppy love affair. I've had so many in the past.

Of course I don't think he knows about it—that I love him. I write him in the professional angle, sometimes just socially. When mother comes to the office with me, he talks to us for a long time about many things. He treats us different than his other patients for he and I have something in common that I can't mention.

He gives the impression that he doesn't like his wife. I've never met the woman. But I believe he is sick of everything. I try so hard to make myself believe that I'm not in love with him, but no can do.

He acts as if he has a great affection for me, but won't say anything because of the circumstances. Should I say it first and maybe settle what we think of each other? Or would I be walking on dangerous territory, also maybe making a chump of myself?

Maybe you can lead me from oncoming disaster.

Jane E.

Dear Miss E:

It is extremely hard for me to judge the situation because of the meager details you have furnished and the things you have left out.

I am sure, if you told this man how you felt, you would always regret it. It would be in extremely bad taste for you to bring up the question of his attitude toward you; when a man of his age has anything he wishes to say to you, rest assured that he will say it, so wait for the time to come.

Bette Davis

Dear Miss Davis:

I'm eighteen-years-old and I feel that my life is just a plain mess. My mother is in the state hospital for mental eases and has been there going on three years. Although I go to see her every single Sunday, I fail to see anything wrong with her.

My brother (I might as well be frank) is in jail going on a year. When I needed him most he failed me and got into trouble and left me to fend for myself. I've spoken to the doctor about my mother and he said that she is perfectly well, but she can't come home until I'm twenty- one. My brother is twenty-one and is serving three-to-six years. If he was home, I'd be able to have my mother taken out.

I'm living with my girl friend's people and they are honestly swell to me. They treat me like their own daughter. I guess you're wondering what I'm getting at.

Here it is: I want to join the Waves. I want to have my own job in the world and do something worthwhile instead of being—well, you know. But if I did that, I couldn't see my Mom every Sunday, and I have no other relatives to send to see her. I know she looks forward to seeing me and listening to me tell her things. When I talked to her about the Waves, she said for me to join. She doesn't know my brother is in the penitentiary - I lied to her and said he had joined the Navy.

I don't mean to sound bitter, but honestly, sometimes I just can't figure out why things happen to people. What can I do, Miss Davis? I don't care what you say—just say something.

Doris K.

Dear Miss K:

I can understand your restlessness to get out and do something, particularly in these times, but your weekly visits must mean a great deal to your mother. After all, you are only eighteen and there will be many years during which you will be able to do the things you want to do.

Your brother, obviously, can be of no help, so you are left with the entire responsibility in this matter, so you must decide it as such.

It seems to me that you are very fortunate in liking the people with whom you are staying; they must have volunteered some advice which you might consider.

You say, at the end of your letters, "sometimes I just can't go figure out why things happen to people..." Remember that, all over the world, things are happening to others that they don't understand either. As a matter of fact, in the lives of those around you there may be many tragic situations of which you don't dream; always remember you aren't the only one with troubles. Maybe this thought will help you over some hurdles in the months to come. I hope so.

Bette Davis

Dear Miss Davis:

I don't know whether men write to you or not, but I am trying, regardless.

My problem is somewhat of a personal nature.

I have been in the Army Air Force eighteen months and I have never gone out with a girl, had a date, and I am self-conscious in front of girls. I have never kissed a girl. I am 20. 5 ft. 11 in. tall, weigh 160, have black hair and brown eyes. I am not too bad-looking except that I have round shoulders. I don't dance, but I sometimes go to the U.S.O clubs for entertainment. I have ambitions to become a radio announcer after the war. How can I develop a smooth-sounding voice, Miss Davis?

As for the problem of girls, what should I do to get a girlfriend? I can talk to them, but the conversation drops off after a while and they seem to lose interest in me. I try to center the attention on them and not to talk about myself. Am I right? Most of my buddies keep late hours, but I don't see the advantage in that. They keep telling me I should go along with them, but I refuse.

My folks never treated me good at all when I was home. That's why I joined the Army.

Does this case sound strange to you, Miss Davis? Please answer and tell me what I should do. I feel lonely and it seems like years since I've had a good time.

Bob Z.

Dear Mr. Z:

I always feel extremely flattered when men write to me about their problems.

Since your "buddies" apparently invite you to go out with them, why don't you ask one why he thinks girls are not into you. Ask him to be entirely frank. He might be able to help you. There is one thing best I can suggest: It would be a good idea for you to learn to dance.

In regards to your ambition to become a radio announcer, why don't you make friends with someone in your camp who has some training in singing? Anyone who has had voice coaching will be able to give you some exercises that will improve your voice.

It all boils down to proper voice placement and proper breathing, and you could certainly be working toward your ultimate goal if you would devote some time to exercises now.

It seems sad to me, and unnecessary, for anyone to feel that it has been years since he has had a good time. I'm sure you can change this if you want to.

Bette Davis

Dear Miss Davis:

I saw your picture, "Now, Voyager," three times. Not only did the acting thrill me, but the music as well. I am a musician in this little town of ten-thousand and I am considered a fairly good pianist. I would like to know the name of the composition that was played while you and Mr. Henreid were alone. First, when you met him on the boat, and when you saw him at the station after the dinner and theater party. It was played mostly by the violins, usually in the high register.

Also I would appreciate it if you would give me the name of the orchestra that may have recorded it

Georgina O.

Dear Miss O:

The song to which you refer was an original love theme composed by Max Steiner and played by the studio orchestra. As you undoubtedly know, it was given an Academy Award. A popular song has been made of the same and titled, "It Can't Be Wrong." I believe that it will soon be available in sheet music, but I haven't yet heard of any orchestras recording it.

Bette Davis

Dear Miss Davis:

I have one of those problems that doesn't seem important to anyone but me.

On my way home from school on the bus one night there was a boy standing fairly close to me and he said to his friend, "I have never seen a good-looking redhead yet."

You see, I am a redhead with a lot of freckles. What can I do to be attractive, so no one will ever say that again?

Evelyn T.

Dear Miss T:

Before you feel too unhappy about this boy's remark, I should like to remind you that practically every girl in the world has wished at some time in her life that she were a red head. I know I have.

Perhaps this particular boy simply wanted to attract your attention and couldn't think of a more tactful way of doing it. It might not have been courteous, but it did get results, as your letter proves. I daresay you would recognize him, no matter where you saw him a second time.

Probably you know that Jeanette MacDonald, Judy Garland, Rita Hayworth, Nancy Coleman, Ann Sheridan and Greer Garson all have red hair. Certainly none of them would fail in a glaucoma test, so cheer up.

Bette Davis

Dear Miss Davis:

I'm so glad you are now giving advice to those who are bewildered in this time of strife. Now, Miss Davis, I have been married fifteen years and I have two lovely girls. My husband has provided me with a good home. We are considered middle class—not able to afford luxuries, but we have nice things. My problem is this: I want to become an airplane mechanic.

Now for the trouble. My husband is in ill health since the last war. He keeps saying he won't live long and I do worry about him. If I don't prepare all his meals I feel I have neglected him and think maybe he isn't getting a balanced diet. He is able to work and keep going, but he says he hasn't much time on this earth and he even told me who he wants to speak at his services. He gave me a few dollars the other day to take to the minister of our church.

Miss Davis, it frightens me, as I want to be with him all I can. When he talks about leaving me and my daughters, I want to scream.

I'd like to get out of the house a little and do something useful like aircraft mechanical work, yet I want to look after my husband. He is everything I ever hoped for in a husband. I know he wants me to be able to carry on, but I think perhaps I should stay as long as possible at my husband's side.

Thank you for your ideas on the subject.

Mrs. Orpha S.

Dear Mrs. S:

I thoroughly appreciate your desire to help your country by becoming an aircraft mechanic, but in your case, your duty is definitely at home with your husband. Knowing how he feels, you would regret every hour you had spent away from him if anything would happen.

Actually, you are doing your bit in the war effort by maintaining a home, as a nation's strength arises from a nation's home. Most of the boys to whom I talk at the Hollywood Canteen are eager to win this war so they can go "back home."

Bette Davis

Dear Miss Davis:

I have only recently been inducted into the Array. Previous to this I was an actor—or thought I was. I did Little Theatre work (twenty-seven plays in about thirty weeks during the last season) and had a dramatic program on the air every Saturday afternoon.

I'm still, even after my induction, as determined as ever to become a great actor, but it is presenting ever-increasing problems. Because of lack of privacy, I hesitate in practicing vocal exercises and recitations. One night I did break down and do Oswald Airing's, "mad" scene from the third act of "Ghosts" and was promptly greeted on all sides by some royal Bronx cheers.

I really don't mind them laughing at me—I'm probably due for a lot more — but I'm afraid I'll go stale from inactivity. Acting is something that must be practiced constantly and I'd hate to lose three years of time and study because of inactivity. I asked permission to put on some plays here at camp, but my suggestion was discarded as "unimportant." What would you suggest I do? Forget about it completely for the time being, or struggle along as I have been completely miserable. Perhaps you'll give me a little help.

Private Joe B.

Dear Private B:

In the first place, it's possible that the "Bronx cheers" were given only because of your selection of material.

I understand very well your fear of going stale from inactivity. If, however, instead of worrying so much about privacy for vocal exercises, you will observe the people with whom you come in contact and learn something of their mannerism and habits of speech, you will be storing up valuable bits of characterization for the future. The war isn't going to last forever, you know, so you can use this time to advantage by increasing your general knowledge and your awareness of the differences in human beings.

For practical exercise, you might volunteer your services to some of the shows that come to your camp, as they always need people of your experience and ability to help out. This will make you feel you are still working at the job you like best.

Bette Davis

Dear Miss Davis:

I'm twenty-two years of age and I never thought that when I married I would have any problems at all.

To begin with, about a year and a half ago, I met a nice man of twenty-eight who came originally from a small town in Massachusetts. He is a draftsman and a college graduate. We discovered in November, last year, that we cared enough to get married, so we did.

Naturally, before I married him. I asked him all about his previous romances. He said that when he was back in his own home he had very little money—going to college and all —so that he hadn't dated very much. But I finally got him to tell me about a nurse he says he had known for about nine years. He swears he never told her he loved her and never proposed, but I can't figure anyone knowing each other that long without getting serious, can you?

I care for my husband, and yet one-hundred-percent do not believe what he tells me of his relationship between this girl and himself. Would it be proper for me to write her and find out just exactly how they felt about each other? She is now married to another man, but I feel that I want the truth about his early life. Am I wrong?

Mrs. Jennifer W.

Dear Mrs W:

I can see no reason for your wanting to find out about the former romantic life of your husband. You remind me of a myth about a girl named Pandora. You probably remember that she was placed in charge of a mysterious box and was warned that it did not belong to her, so she must never open it. But Pandora was made restless by the gnawing of curiosity, so she opened the box... thereby releasing, "All the troubles in the world."

Your problem boils down to this: Your husband has married you, so what difference does it make what he did before, as long as you are happily married now? Why go into ancient history?

You would subject yourself to severe criticism if you wrote to this girl and ask for her version of his alleged romance. How do you think your husband would feel about such a letter? At the expense of sounding very trite, I must say - let bygones be bygones.

Bette Davis

Dear Miss Davis:

You have been so helpful to other girls with problems, so perhaps you can help me.

I am twenty-three and a bookkeeper in a department store. My father has bad health and never will be able to work regularly again. He doesn't make much from part-time jobs so my family looks to me for financial aid. I turn most of my money over to them. I have a younger sister who is just starting high school so she won't be out for four years.

I have broken up with most of the boys I have dated because I know how impossible it is for me to marry and leave home. I am going with a nice boy now. I think he will ask me to marry him soon. You know a girl can always tell when a boy is getting serious. If I let myself, I could love him very much as he is really wonderful.

Should I break off with him before our romance goes any further? My friends advise me to marry and let my family get along the best they can, but I hate to hurt them. Sometimes I think I'll have to be an old maid.

Jane A.

P. S. Will you please send me the name and address of the little girl who was so short and who had no boyfriends. I would like her to get in touch with me so I could give her some suggestions and ideas that worked wonders for me. I was like her once. I am only four-feet-ten and one-half inches tall myself.

J. A

Dear Miss A:

When this boy asked you to marry him, why don't you explain the situation fully?

If he really loves you, he will agree with you that you must carry on your responsibilities. But there is no reason - if he is working, which I presume he is - why you can't also have a life of your own. You could continue to give financial aid at home, while he supports the two of you.

There is no woman so lonely as one who has sacrificed her entire life for her family and then - when the parents have passed away and the younger children have married - finds herself stranded without emotional ties.

I am mailing you, under separate cover, the information that you wanted about the small girl. It is generous of you to volunteer to help.

Bette Davis

Dear Miss Davis:

I'm a girl of eighteen, all ready to get married with one exception. I need advice and I need it bad. I have no one to turn to, so I'm begging you for help.

I have a stepmother; my real mother died when I was about two-weeks-old; my grandmother took care of me from then until I was eleven.

I know this isn't nice to say, but it's the truth: I hate my stepmother and my father for the simple reason that they've ruined my life. When I was eleven, my stepmother decided she wanted a child and she thought I'd be in the way at such a time. She treated me horribly, made me stay outside in rainy weather until my father came home from work. The neighbors began to talk, but she didn't care—she knew I'd do something to give her reason to put me away. I did. I ran away—that's what she called it, although I only went to my grandmother's.

My stepmother had me put in an institution the next day. It hurt me so to know that my dad would let her do it. I had been at the home six years when my stepmother decided she wanted someone to do her housework and take care of the baby, so she took me out of the institution.

She had me put on parole until I'm twenty-one, so she could have me sent back at any time. The abuse I took? She threw things at me and hit me with anything she happened to have in her hands. I couldn't take it any longer so I ran away again. She reported it, but the home—instead of taking me back—made my grandmother my guardian and let me live with her.

My stepmother was so mad she wouldn't let Dad give us any money, so we had to go on relief. Granny had a stroke a few weeks later and died.

Well, one of the officers from the home came to see me and told me I had my choice: Go back to the home, or live with my stepmother and father. I wanted neither, so I did the only thing I could think of: I ran away again. I came West— almost a year now. I still don't have any peace because my stepmother notified the police. She wants me back in that home, but I'll die first. I'm sorry I had to tell you all this - but you've got to know what I'm up against.

Now, about George. I've been going with him eight months. He wants to marry me, even though he knows all about my family. He's good, kind and decent; I think the world of him. But if I marry him, it might make some sort of trouble for him. I'm not supposed to marry without the home's permission.

I keep putting him off all the time because I'm half-crazy, not knowing what to do. Where can I go for advice, without getting into trouble—except to you?

Ruth T.

Dear Miss T:

I consulted my own attorney about your case and he suggested that the only thing for you to do is to look through the telephone book (the yellow section) and find the address and telephone of the State Bar Association in the state in which you are living at present. Ask them to tell you how to get to their Legal Aid Clinics, which will advise you without charge.

Naturally, the easiest thing to do would be to consult your attorney near you, what I understand there might be a financial problem and Legal Aid Clinics, you know, give official advice without charge.

This should be a comfort to you and encourage you to see any attorney and get everything straightened out. I understand that it is the habit in most states (particularly in the one in which you are now living) to parole a girl to her husband when she marries. In this way, marriage to this boy would solve all your problems at once.

Bette Davis

From Canada comes this letter:

Dear Miss Davis:

I am sixteen years of age and I am going to business college. I shall soon finish my course, but instead of going into an office as a clerk, I want to join the Woman's Army.

My parents object to this notion very much. They think that I am too young. They say that, considering my two brothers' being in the Royal Air Force, that is enough of the family to be fighting at present.

What do you think I should do?

Ever your friend.

M.

Dear Miss M.:

There can, of course, be no doubt in anyone's mind of the worthlessness of the Woman's Auxiliaries to any of the services; American, Canadian or British. However, whether you join or not must be, obviously, a completely personal decision. Since I know none of the circumstances that surround your life, I can't direct you, either toward service or toward office work you mention.

Perhaps the objection of your parents to your joining is based, somewhat, on fear for your safety. Then, too, during wartime, parents are likely to cling to the child who can be kept at home.

Perhaps your greatest service to your country at this time lies in keeping your parents happy and keeping your home the same as your fighting brothers remember.

Yours truly,

Bette Davis

Dear Miss Davis:

I have been very much impressed by your answers to the serious problems in Photoplay-Movie Mirror, so now I am bringing you my troubles in the hope that you can help me. So far I've asked advice from no one and it is with great modesty that I now ask you.

I am a very attractive girl of twenty whose parents won't allow me to go out with boys. Almost every boy I meet asks me for a date, but I have to refuse all of them. Naturally, they don't believe me when I say my parents won't allow me to have dates.

I don't care to go out with everyone I meet, but I think now that I've met the most important man in my life, I think I will love him forever. I have never had a date with him—just talked to him in the office and that is all. I am afraid to let him come to the house for fear my parents will make a fuss and disgrace me.

Sometimes I wish I were homely so no one would ever look at me and then I would be satisfied to stay home night after night, like I do now. But I'm not satisfied even if my being at home does make my parents happy.

I have tried to talk this over sensibly with my parents, but it's no use. They say no decent girl goes out with boys. Should I listen to my parents all my life, or should I go ahead and do what I think is best for my own future happiness?

Yours truly.

A.

Dear Miss A:

Of course it is not true that, "no decent girl goes out with boys." It is right and normal for any girl to want beaus.

Frankly, I think your parents were very wise to protect you until you were eighteen. I personally believe that all girls should have their early escorts checked by their families and that most social activities should be home parties.

I remember very well how infuriated I used to be because my mother brought me up in exactly this way. I wanted, like you, to go out with boys just as other girls did.

However, I do feel that after a girl is eighteen she should be allowed more freedom. No parent is going to be able to make decisions for his children forever; young people have to learn to cope with problems of adult life as they meet them.

At twenty, I think a girl should certainly be given some choice in the matter and should be able to choose beaus intelligently; or else it seems to me her parents' upbringing has been inadequate.

I feel, honestly, that for you to abide by so strict a rule as that laid down by your parents at present may endanger your future happiness.

Yours truly,
Bette Davis

Dear Miss Davis:

I am a girl, fifteen, but I feel at least ten years older. Here is my problem: My father and I both have very hot tempers. I don't get along with him at all.

He won't let me go anywhere without a big argument. Why? I can't even go to the corner drugstore without having him send my kid brother after me. If I had ever done anything to deserve all this suspicion, I wouldn't mind, but I have always been decent and I intend to stay that way.

One of the things that is wrong with him is that he gambles all the time— plays the ponies. He comes in the door arguing and he goes out of the door arguing. He is always mad about something. I get along swell with my mother who is a darling person. My parents are still young; my father is only thirty-six and my mother is only thirty-four.

My mother works hard to keep our house nice, but she never gets any thanks. I work after school, and all day Saturdays, so that I can buy all my own school clothes.

Please. Miss Davis, can you tell me any way to get a happy home life for my mother and me?

Yours truly,

L

Dear Miss L.:

I'm very much afraid that your father's conduct is not your problem; it is your mother's responsibility.

There is very little that you can do about the situation, it seems to me, until you are of age. Then, if your home life is still too uncomfortable, you can get a job and live apart from your parents.

Here is one fact I think you might consider: The only way human beings can live together with any success is to adapt themselves to conditions. Differences of temperament are very usual in most families. I don't think there is any doubt that your mother loves your father and I think you must love him, too, or you wouldn't be so worried about his behavior.

Don't make yourself miserable over his shortcomings. Remember his good qualities, and he must have many or your mother wouldn't have married him since she is such a "darling person."

Yours truly,
Bette Davis

Dear Miss Davis:

I am only a little girl, but maybe you will answer my letter anyway.

When Daddy gives me my allowance I buy Defense Stamps with half of it and the rest I use for movies. I go to the show every day after school, except on Tuesdays when I have my piano and dancing lessons. Daddy doesn't get home from work until six o'clock. My mother died when I was born and then we lived with Grandma until she died.

Miss Davis, here is my problem. I went to a movie and saw "Blossoms In The Dust." Greer Garson was the mother in it and I love her. I saw it three times, then I saw "Mrs. Miniver" five times.

I am saving every penny I can get and then I am coming to Hollywood to see Miss Garson. I am not telling Daddy because I don't think he would let me go, but, Miss Davis, I simply have to see her. Don't you think it would be all right for me to go to see her?

Yours lovingly,

Janie.

Dear Janie:

I can well understand your admiration for Miss Garson, as she is one of the most beautiful and charming women I have ever met.

However, I believe I have a better plan for you than coming to Hollywood. Nearly every Star is now doing a great deal of war work, going on Bond tours, or traveling from camp to camp entertaining soldiers. It is entirely possible that Miss Garson will appear in your town or one nearby.

Why don't you watch the papers for news of her visit? Then you could have your father take you to see her and spare you both the long trip to Hollywood.

You forgot to put your address in your letter, but if you will send it to me I will (just for you) ask Miss Garson for a photograph and mail it to you.

Sincerely yours,
Bette Davis

Dear Miss Davis:

I always read Photoplay-Movie Mirror and I was very interested to learn that you are acting as consultant for its readers. I have a very serious problem.

My husband and I were married when I was twenty and he was twenty-five—we were both old enough to know our own minds and we were very much in love. Still, his mother didn't approve of me. She made the statement that my family were not her equals. She wouldn't even have me in her house and when my baby daughter was born she didn't send flowers, or telephone to find out how I was, or even visit our flat to see how my husband was getting along while I was in the hospital.

My little girl was only three when we moved out of our home state because my husband, George, wanted to change his type of work. We had some pretty tough times, I can tell you. Lots of times we didn't know where the next meal was coming from, but somehow we managed without calling on George's mother. I've always been a good manager and George could always bring in an odd dollar when things got desperate. For five years we were strangers to George's people.

Then one day I met George's brother on the street. I was astonished and so was he. I invited him home to have dinner with us and he said he and my mother-in-law were living only a few blocks down the street. Well. I can't say I was happy about it, but what could I do? At Thanksgiving time I invited George's brother and mother over for dinner and we sort of patched things up. Still, she has never invited me to set foot in her house. That went on for three years.

This summer she begged me to let Joan, my daughter, stay with her while George and I took a little vacation. I wanted Joan to go along with us, but George thought it would be fun to have a second honeymoon and to leave Joan with her grandmother, which we did.

Well, when we came home, Joan told me that her

grandmother had spent the entire time ridiculing me and telling stories about my family. My mother-in-law made fun of my clothes, of my house—well, of everything about me to my own daughter.

Now, Miss Davis, I think I would be justified in breaking off all relations with George's mother. I think I should never telephone her again, and never see her, also that I should keep Joan away from her.

George doesn't feel that way. He says we have to make allowances for older people and that it isn't fair to keep the only grandchild away from her grandmother.

How can I stand to go on sitting for hours in the same room with a woman who is mentally jeering at me? How can I risk her turning Joan against me? My family are all dead now, so there is no way that I can show Joan that I really came from nice, if plain people.

What shall I do, Miss Davis?

Unhappily yours,

J.

Dear Mrs. J.:

I sincerely agree with you when you say that you have a difficult problem. In the first place, your husband has a point when he says that we have to make allowances for older people. Your husband is also right when he says that a grandchild is important to its grandmother.

But you are right in resenting anything that comes between you and your daughter, as it is important for her to grow up to respect you. Anyone who attempts to undermine the affection and reverence of a child for its mother is, of course, in the wrong.

Personally, I feel that your husband should stand by you in preference to his mother in this matter, but undoubtedly he loves his mother and feels loyalty for her.

I feel that, already, you are definitely justified in breaking off all relations with your husband's mother, but if you love your husband - which you seem to - why not have one more try?

Go and discuss with your mother-in-law her attitude toward you and ask her quite frankly what does she hope to gain by turning your daughter against you? Very often the most difficult situations can be cleared up if the people themselves sit down and talk about it.

It seems to me this is your only hope. In doing this, you are being fair to everyone involved, and no one can say you haven't done everything in your power to keep peace in the family.

Yours truly,
Bette Davis

Dear Miss Davis:

My boyfriend is 23, and I have been going with him for the past year. We became engaged after we had known each other 8 months. I inquired—after we were engaged—why he was in Class 4F. He told me of a scrape he was in when he was just 17; he stole a car.

Previous to the time I met him he had been in the Army for five months, but was discharged because he had lied about this felony on his record. Now, well over a year after Pearl Harbor, he still hasn't been drafted. It began to seem odd to me, because another boy in our town—who had a record—was drafted. Because of my insistence that George find out about his status, he told me of a second felony.

Here's my question: Even if I love him (which I really do) can I accept the situation as it is and marry him?

He says that he loves me so much that if anything should happen between us, he just wouldn't be responsible for what would happen.

I've rather wanted to join the WAAC ever since they organized and I think that might be a way out for me. After all, a woman wants to be proud of her future husband.

Please, Miss Davis, since I love him so desperately, should I marry him and face this, or should I join up and work out my heartache for my country?

Jean C.

Dear Miss C:

It seems impossible to me, judging from your letter, that you could be really proud of this boy.

Of course, what your problem boils down to is this: Which is more important to you - what a boy has been or has done in the past, or what he is going to be in the future? You have known him long enough to tell whether he has overcome the things in his character that caused his collusion with the law in the first place.

If he hasn't, I certainly would advise you against marrying him to try to reform him. It never works.

As I have said before in some of my answers, this is a problem so individual and containing so many details of which I know nothing, that it must be decided by you alone.

Bette Davis

Dear Miss Davis:

I know you are very busy, so I'll get right to the point.

I am not ugly and I'm not beautiful: I guess I'm just in-between, but I have one great disadvantage. Here is the 'lowdown." When I was six-years-old, I was hit by an automobile. Now I have a scar in the middle of my forehead which extends down near my eyes.

I've been in many plays and sung on many programs in school (I am now fourteen) and every time I appear, I want more and more to be a singer. But my friends laugh at me. I cry myself to sleep almost every night.

Do you think I should give up my hopes because of my problem?

Josette G.

Dear Miss G:

It is a little difficult for me to give you an honest opinion, as I have no way of knowing - from your letter - just how noticeable your scar is. In case it is extremely noticeable, it seems to me that you should consider plastic surgery when you are older. Remarkable things are being done in this field.

However, at present I believe you could make your life pleasanter if you would consistently use one of the heavier powder bases on the market. The cosmetics buyer in any store in your town will be able to recommend one of these. If your scar is not a bad one, it wouldn't inhibit a career for you, as makeup covers a multitude of sins.

Yours sincerely,
Bette Davis

Dear Miss Davis:

I turn to you with my problem as I know you to be a very understanding person. I had the great pleasure of meeting you in New Hampshire at the premiere of, "The Great Lie," and talking to you for some time—not that I expect you to remember me as you meet so many people of really great importance.

I am nineteen, and I am engaged to a very nice young man who is twenty- two. He is an officer in the armed forces. I have known this boy for five years; ever since high-school days. He is a fine man, comes from a very nice family, and is a graduate of M.I.T.

When I told my parents we were going to be married, they said I should wait until the war is over and then perhaps they would approve. I am so very much in love with him and he with me that we feel we are right in marrying and we hope to have what little happiness we can together, before he goes abroad.

My parents have informed me that if I marry against their wishes, they will turn me out of the house for good and that when he goes overseas, I shall have to find somewhere to go. Also, not to bother them ever again. My in-laws-to-be are very fond of me and approve of the marriage. They have said that I may live with them when the time presents itself.

I don't want to break with my parents, but I love this boy very much and I feel that I am old enough to be married. Miss Davis, what shall I do?

Margaret T.

Dear Miss T:

Legally, as you probably know, a girl of nineteen has the privilege to marry whom and when she likes. However, I have always believed that one should, as far as is humanly possible, act in accordance with one's parents' wishes.

I think that if you would have another talk with your parents, asking them to consider the strange times in which we are living and explaining to them that you don't want to marry without their consent, they might change their minds.

If they refuse, you are faced with a problem that only you can solve. Your parents can't judge how much you love this boy, nor how much you are willing to sacrifice for him. As for the boy, does he know that your parents oppose your marriage? If so, does he know why? Be sure, before you decide, that he is fully aware of the whole situation, then work out the problem with him.

Sincerely,
Bette Davis

Dear Miss Davis:

I have been married for two years. My husband is a farmer but I had always lived in the city until I was married.

All this time I have lived on the farm and tried my best to make my husband happy! But now it has come to a place where I can't possibly stand it any longer as we live with his father and I cannot get along with him at all.

I have begged my husband and yes, even threatened to leave him, if he wouldn't move off the farm and try to get himself a defense job as I hear there are plenty—and well paid. He says that his place is on the farm and he will never leave it as his sisters and his father depend upon him.

There was a mutual understanding at the time of our marriage that we would live anywhere I chose. My opinion is that he is afraid of being drafted if he leaves the farm.

Would you leave him and get a divorce if you had a good home to return to, as I have, or would you stay with him on the farm and continue to make unheard- of-sacrifices? I don't believe we will ever get ahead, as his dad controls all the money.

Emily Anne B.

Dear Mrs. B:

Evidently you no longer love your husband, because when one is in love one wants to be with that person all the time - regardless of where he is.

No woman, if a man loves a particular occupation, has the right to demand that he give it up because of her. Even if he promised to live in a city when he asked you to marry him, he probably now realizes this would not be right for him. I'm sure he thought you would grow to love the home he made for you.

None of us who has just finished signing up for food ration books can look upon a good, sincere, hard-working farmer with anything but the highest respect and admiration.

Sincerely,
Bette Davis

Dear Miss Davis:

In reading your column, I've noticed that quite a few girls complain about their appearance and ask you to give them advice on how to become more attractive.

Sometimes I don't think average-looking girls realize how lucky they are. I recently secured a position with a coal company in the office. I have worked a long time, and studied, to equip myself for this job. I have twelve men working for me, but unless I can find an answer to my puzzle, I may have to give it up.

You see, everyone tells me I am exceptionally good-looking. I have never considered this important as I have always wanted to improve my mind. But to get to my difficulty: The first few weeks of my new job were very pleasant; the men were co-operative and courteous.

Then, in the next few weeks they began to hang around the office and carry on silly chatter. I couldn't get my work out because the men were just too friendly. In desperation I went to my employer and told him of the situation. He laughed and said he couldn't fire twelve men; that he would just have to lose me if the men wouldn't stay out of the office.

I have worked so hard to get this position and I like it so well that I can't bear to give it up. But what can I do without being mean and making enemies?

Helene S.

Dear Miss S:

Under no condition give up a position that you have worked for, and honestly, one that you like.

Part of your difficulty is caused, no doubt, by the celebrated habit of girls who say "no" and really mean "yes." Your very indifference and concentration on your work are probably interpreted as part of some enticing new technique.

In your favor is the fact that men are apt to become discouraged if they find a girl isn't interested. It isn't necessary for you to be unpleasant or to make enemies to accomplish this. Simply be tactful and firm. Ask them calmly to stay out of the office because you have work to do. If you are nice about it, and if your tone and attitude are absolutely impersonal, I feel sure these men will - in the long run - believe you and respect you for your attitude.

Sincerely yours,

Bette Davis

Dear Miss Davis:

I'm just at the point where I don't know what to do.

When I was 19 (I am now 21) I was married. You see, my mother is Russian and she believes that if you aren't married by 20, you're disgracing the family. She really had me believing that no one would ever want me, so when I met this boy, I married him just to satisfy her, although I knew I didn't love him.

We just didn't get along from the very first. When I knew I was going to have a baby, I thought it would make everything right, but it didn't. Miss Davis, my baby was born with water on the brain and it only lived a month. When the baby died, my husband left me, saying I was no good as a woman.

Then my mother started again, also saying I was no good and that I should have died instead of my father. You see, I was six when he and I were in a car together and we had an accident. He died and now she's forever telling me it should have been me.

My mother isn't very well and I have tried to take care of her, but I don't think I can stand it much longer. What would you do? Try to turn a deaf ear to her nagging, or go to some other town and get a job and start life fresh without my family?

Tania M.

Dear Miss M:

As you said yourself, your mother obviously isn't very well and I am sure this must partly excuse her actions.

Certainly you weren't in the least responsible for the death of your father and you shouldn't be harried and made miserable because of it. Neither are you responsible for the death of your child, nor does this unusual condition reflect any discredit upon your womanhood. Both were utterly beyond your power to change.

Your husband and your mother have been entirely wrong in goading you into your present state of misery. I never advocate leaving a mother, but in your case, it would seem that your only chance for salvation lies in starting out on your own.

Sincerely yours,

Bette Davis

Dear Miss Davis:

I have read somewhere that you are head of the U.S.O., and I wondered if you were the person who made the rule that girls under eighteen can't enter U.S.O. centers?

I am seventeen and my boyfriend is stationed near the town where I live. Really, there aren't many places around here where decent people can go and have a nice time. The U.S.O workers are always giving parties for soldiers and inviting a lot of girls, but we girls sixteen and seventeen get turned down at the door. We are embarrassed to death.

My boyfriend has to take an older girl to these parties and I am left out. Can't something be done about it? It seems like a silly rule—what difference does a year make?

Won't you please look into it and try to get that rule repealed?

Grace B.

Dear Miss B:

I am extremely flattered to learn that you think I am head of U.S.O, as I am hardly equipped for this job, which is a colossal one.

These rules are made and enforced by the U.S.O. chairman in each community, I understand. So the only thing for you to do is to take it up with your local U.S.O.

Sincerely,

Bette Davis

Dear Miss Davis:

I am a bride of six months and have a very dear husband. We love each other deeply. He has had a very difficult life as he has worked since he was fourteen. Now, he has a rather important job and we get along very nicely on his salary.

After two months of marriage, he brought up the subject of a wife's being independent. He wants me to go to school and to learn to be something. He says that he has seen so many changes concerning work that he feels a woman should be able to share in supporting a home, if need be.

I love being a housewife and I know I would be very unhappy if I had to go to work. I like to cook, and clean, and have my home attractive. How can a woman keep up with household duties when she has to go off to the office? I told him a girl marries to have someone to depend on.

Do you believe a woman has to learn to be self-supporting?

Patricia J.

Dear Mrs. J:

I happen to agree with your husband. I think that every human being should be self-supporting. Who knows what the future may bring, or of what great value trained women may be in the post-war world.

I, personally, have a pretty big job to do, yet I managed to do lots of things in my own home in spare time snatched after working hours.

It seems to me that you are fortunate to have the sort of husband you do. After all, housework for the first six months is fun, but after four or five years of it, it fails to satisfy you all day, everyday.

Also, I believe you will find that learning to become self-supporting will bring something new and very interesting into your life.

Sincerely
Bette Davis

Dear Miss Bette:

I met a man who is fifty-two and was a doctor in Vienna. He has two lovely boys ten and twelve years—Sascha and Joe. The doctor was in a concentration camp and is very much broken up. His wife died in France.

He is here only two years and just made his state exam as a doctor. If he passed he'll find a home for the boys who are in a boarding school now.

I suggested in the summer, when I was camp nurse and he was camp doctor, that he should marry a rich woman and I would be governess to the boys and help in the office. Well, now it seems we like each other and the boys adore me.

But this worries me—is there a late luck for a woman when she is an old maid nearing fifty? Is there any happiness for me, or am I maybe a silly old fool to fall in love with him, and him with me?

Dora W.

Dear Miss W:

There is certainly no reason why, even though you are nearing fifty, you should consider yourself an old maid. It is entirely possible for people of all ages to fall in love and marry; you must have heard the saying that a person is only as old as he feels.

There is a Swiss legend that tells how the crocus - a symbol of Awakening vitally - always blooms twice, once in spring and once in the fall.

Certainly, there is nothing in the least ridiculous in a mature love.

Sincerely yours,
Bette Davis

Dear Miss Davis:

I may never mail this letter, but I am being driven to write to you by an urge that I can't understand. Probably I have a great many peculiar urges—to judge from what I am going to tell you.

For several years since my parents' death I have lived alone in a small house.

I was given every advantage of Christian training as a child. I have a good education, too—something that, in the getting, caused my parents to sacrifice many personal comforts.

After I recovered from my first horrible grief at my parents' death, I picked myself up and went back to my teaching position. One of my pupils was a beautiful brown-eyed boy of ten, bright, laughing and friendly. But he had one very serious fault: He had no sense of property rights at all. If any of the children missed an article, I always knew where to find it. When I scolded him he would look up at me in astonishment and say, "But I wanted it! I thought it was pretty!"

Now, this is the crazy thing that happened to me—and to be honest, I don't know what Tommy and his failing had to do with it, but I was in a dime store one day and saw a bright red hair ribbon bow. I simply picked it up and walked out.

That was only the beginning. In spite of myself, I began to pick up all sorts of odd and useless things. This has been going on for two years. When I look in the drawers of Mother's dresser, I shudder to realize what I am doing.

But that isn't the end of my woes by a long margin. I was caught out in a sudden rain last summer and two radio officers brought me home. One of them came back a day or so later to return a school notebook I had left in the back of the car, and we became friends. Now that friendship has become love, pure and simple, and he wants me to marry him.

I guess I don't need to go on. If you're laughing, I don't blame you. I laugh rather wryly myself sometimes.

Well, Miss Davis, where do we go from here? What shall I do? Tell him the truth and lose him; or marry him and disgrace him by being caught eventually and branded . . . well, I can't write the word, it's too awful.

Gareth M.

Dear Miss M:

In the first place, your condition is nothing of your own choosing. I have learned that these things are not disgraceful, any more than whooping cough is, because they, too, can be cured.

Of course, you must tell this man the full truth about your trouble. If he is the right kind of person, he will be able to help you. If he isn't the right kind of person, you might as well know it before you marry him instead of afterward.

I would also suggest that you go and talk this over with a psychiatrist. Don't try to solve your problem alone. And, above all - don't think that you are a disgrace to anyone - you aren't!

Sincerely yours,

Bette Davis

Editor's Note: As Bette Davis has written you in her own words reproduced on this page, this must be the last issue in which she gives her answers to the questions sent her by Photoplay readers.

It is with the most sincere regret that the editors permit her to withdraw from this association which has meant so much to the magazine, but with the conclusion that you will understand the necessity.

Beginning next month an entirely new kind of page will be created where readers can come for counsel and inspiration. To Bette Davis goes credit for originating this page in Photoplay; to the editors will go the responsibility for maintaining in future months the high reader interest and integrity of service the page has offered under Bette's guidance.

F. R. S.

Epilogue

* *"...BY RACIAL ACCIDENT OF BIRTH."*

Although I love Bette Davis, she was still a product of her time. This statement was racist. Being born a, "minority" should not be considered, "an accident of birth."

About The Author

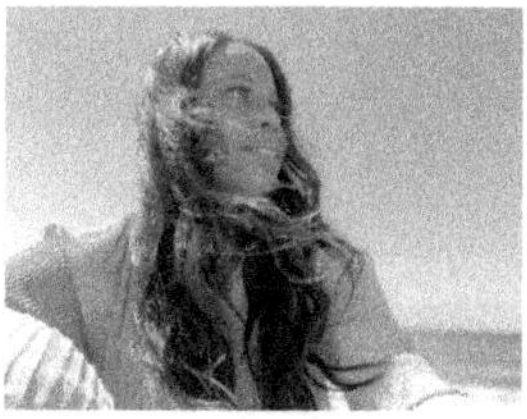

Patrice Williams Marks is a screenwriter, author of fiction and how-to books, a Sensitivity Reader, founder of courses that teach Sensitivity Reading and founder of a non-profit charity. She also has a background in public relations, marketing, and journalism with an emphasis on research.

Reach Out:
www.PatriceWilliamsMarks.com
pwm@patricewilliamsmarks.com

Reviews welcome and appreciated on all platforms.

tiktok.com/@booksbypatrice
twitter.com/PWilliamsMarks
youtube.com/PatriceWilliamsMarks
facebook.com/Author.PatriceWilliamsMarks
instagram.com/patricewilliamsmarks

CPSIA information can be obtained
at www.ICGtesting.com
Printed in the USA
LVHW010347010422
714933LV00011B/1379

9 798201 357047